UNRAVELING
THE ORIGINS
CONTROVERSY

D0115478

UNRAVELING
THE ORIGINS
CONTROVERSY

DAVID A. DEWITT, PH.D.

First printing: June 2007

Cover design Matthew Berman

Unraveling the Origins Controversy
Copyright © 2007 by David A. DeWitt, Ph.D. All rights reserved.
No part of this book may be used or reproduced in any manner
whatsoever without written permission from the publisher with the
exception of brief quotations for articles and reviews. Published
by Creation Curriculum, L.L.C., P.O. Box 4662, Lynchburg, VA
24502 USA

Scripture taken from the HOLY BIBLE, NEW
INTERNATIONAL VERSION. Copyright © 1973, 1978, 1984
International Bible Society. Used by permission of Zondervan
Bible Publishers.

ISBN: 9780979632303
Library of Congress Control Number: 2007903319

Printed in the United States of America

Please visit us at www.creationcurriculum.com
For information: info@creationcurriculum.com

CREATI●N
CURRICULUM LLC

*This book is dedicated to my loving wife, Marci,
and our wonderful daughters:
Kathleen, Emily and Sarah.*

*In memory of:
Dr. Jerry Falwell
1933-2007*

Acknowledgements:

I would like to thank my good friends and colleagues who helped review this book including Daniel Howell, Ph.D., Eugene Sattler, Ph.D., Marcus Ross, Ph.D., Harvey Hartman, Th.D., Jason Lisle, Ph.D., Evangelos Skoumbourdis, Ed.D., Jonathan Falwell, Will Honeycutt, Frank Walters, and Ken Ham. I would also like to thank my CRST 390 students who read an early draft of the book.

I have had many others whose contributions, prayers and encouragement helped make this book possible including George Young, Paul Sattler, Ph.D., J. Doug Oliver, Ph.D., all of my colleagues in the Department of Biology & Chemistry, Edward Edmond and his VCAR 341 class, Steve Deckard, Ed.D., Nena Fox and Michael Wilson.

Most importantly, I would like to thank R. Terry Spohn, Ph.D. who has been both a professional and spiritual mentor to me for over a decade. The valuable discussions, encouragement, and prayers were instrumental in shaping my views on the origins controversy

Table of Contents

Preface

"In the beginning, God created the heavens and the earth."
Genesis 1:1 (NIV)

Few statements are as profound as the opening sentence of the Bible. Yet in our day, this simple truth is both controversial and confusing. Some will argue that science has eliminated the need for God to explain origins and that evolution is a proven scientific fact. Others believe that God was involved but that he used evolutionary processes to "create" the first man and woman. Still others contend that the creation account in Genesis represents an accurate, historical account. Everyone else is somewhere in between these views.

The creation/evolution debate is not science vs. religion or fact vs. faith but a battle over interpretation. The facts do not speak for themselves; they are interpreted within a framework. That framework not only determines the conclusions that will be reached, but also the types of questions that will be asked in the first place. In many cases then, the assumptions that one starts with direct the outcomes that will be reached. Since those assumptions—whether evolution or creation—cannot be proven, both are taken on faith. The key is to find out which assumptions are valid and which are not.

I have taken an approach that is based on *presuppositional apologetics*. Presuppositional apologetics seeks to defend the foundational beliefs and premises of Scripture while challenging alternatives. Therefore, much of the evidence that is often discussed in the context of the origins controversy has been purposefully excluded. Instead, arguments and evidence are used to support or challenge presuppositions rather than to prove the case with evidence alone.

The book begins with the importance of worldview and distinguishes between historical and empirical science. Biblical issues are then addressed to lay a foundation that is firmly rooted in the Word of God. From there, the scientific aspects are tackled from natural selection and the big bang theory to human origins and the origin of life.

The information in this book will be of little value if it is not shared with others. That is why the last chapter focuses on "creation evangelism" and how to use origins in helping others understand the Gospel of Jesus Christ. My purpose in writing this book has been to encourage people to trust what the Word of God says. In so doing, we can all be better witnesses of the glorious salvation that we have in Christ. It is my sincere prayer that the reader will be encouraged in faith and better able to defend what they believe about the origin of life. For those who have doubts about Biblical creation, I hope that they will seriously consider the arguments presented in this book.

David A. DeWitt, Ph.D.

1

What Difference Does a Worldview Make?

Alice: Would you tell me, please, which way I ought to go from here?
The Cat: That depends a good deal on where you want to get to.
Alice: I don't much care where.
The Cat: Then it doesn't much matter which way you go
Lewis Carroll
Alice in Wonderland

A Trip to Washington, D.C.

On Constitution Avenue, between the Capitol and the Washington Monument is the National Museum of Natural History of the Smithsonian Institution. Like the other museums on the Mall in Washington, D.C., this museum is impressive even from the outside. In the spring of 2006, I took a group of college students on a field trip to visit this museum and its many exhibits. I wanted them to see their tax dollars at work and how the theory of evolution is promoted at the museum.

As you walk into the central area of the museum, in the middle of the Rotunda is a huge (stuffed) African elephant. On either side of the Rotunda are very large halls. On one side, you catch a glimpse of a dinosaur skeleton; evolution will surely be promoted

13

there. On the other side is the Hall of Mammals, a long, wide, well lit corridor with stuffed examples of a wide range of mammals. As you enter this room, the tall giraffe is the first animal that catches your eye. 'What amazing creatures might await us inside!' you ponder with enthusiasm.

But that is when you notice the large sign that reads:

Welcome to the mammal family reunion!
Come meet your relatives.

As you tour the wide range of exhibits, from aardvark to zebra, from dingo to lion, and from walrus to bat, it becomes clear that the purpose of the entire hall is to promote evolution. Rather than emphasizing the characteristics that make each creature unique, every sign promotes evolution with "related to", "millions of years", and "adapted to". There can be no doubt that the purpose of the exhibit is to reinforce belief in evolution.

Evolution is used as a verb. One sign reads, "As mammals adapted to a changing world, a wondrous diversity of shapes, sizes and behaviors evolved." Although the general process of evolution is explained, one notices a lack of evidence *demonstrating* the process. For example, the giraffe supposedly evolved from ancestors with short necks because its long neck enabled it to eat leaves from tall trees. However, the "short-necked giraffe" is not a giraffe at all, but an okapi. One wonders what the baby long necked giraffe would eat and how the okapi managed to survive if only leaves on tall trees were available for food. Which mutations were responsible for developing the long neck? How did the giraffe also get one way restrictive valves in arteries to reduce blood pressure when it bends over to get a drink? These and other questions are ignored in favor of blanket statements of the "fact" of evolution.

Evolution is also used as a noun. "Evolution at work" is the heading on a sign at the front of the museum. "Evolution is the biological process responsible for the magnificent diversity of life on Earth. Over time, evolution creates new species." Yes, the sign really says that *evolution creates.*

14

Toward the back of the Hall, there are four large rectangular pillars arranged in a tight formation. Carved on each pillar are the words "From One Ancestor, Many Mammals." There is also an invitation to "Meet One of Your Oldest Relatives." As you walk into this shrine for the "oldest mammal ancestor," you notice the bronze object on the small wooden pedestal in the center. The object looks like a tiny rat or mole. However, it is neither. It is a **Morganucodon**, an extinct, insect-eating mammal. While we were there examining the idol, a boy about 6 years old asked his mom about the bronze "rat". "That is our oldest mammal relative," the parent dutifully read, passing on to her child the collective wisdom of the scientific elite.

In back of the "ancestor shrine" is the "Evolution Theater" with a continuously playing movie. The movie is fast paced and geared toward children. Not everyone is invited to the "mammal family reunion". Fish aren't, frogs aren't, and neither are birds. In order to be invited, you need hair, special ear bones, and a mother that makes milk. The main characters in the movie are "Harry", a chimpanzee, and the morganucodon that we can call "Great grandma Morgie"

Man is significantly downplayed in the movie. If the whole period of time that mammals existed on earth were compressed to one hour, humans would come on the scene in the very last second. Everything is continuously changing, especially the environment. In order to survive, mammals have to adapt. That requires "time, genes, and a little luck." At the end of the movie, we are invited back with a teaser: "Who knows what new mammals we might see at the next mammal family reunion!"

In the museum gift shop, you can purchase an IMAX film on DVD with the title, *GENESIS: Fourteen billion years in the making.* Or if books are your thing, *Evolving Eden* is an option. In spite of the Biblical sounding titles, these are evolution materials with no mention of creation or God.

The take home message is obvious. Scientists have worked out all of the problems and can explain how the earth began, the origin of life and the source of all of its diversity. When it comes to origins, there is no doubt, no question and no controversy.

Scientists have everything figured out. Evolution is a fact, fact, fact, and there is no place for religion or the divine.

But if you take a walk across the street from the museum, you can visit the National Archives. On display in this museum is an original, signed copy of the Declaration of Independence. Here, you can read those immortal words penned by Thomas Jefferson:

> "We hold these truths to be self evident: that all men are created equal, that they are endowed by their Creator with certain unalienable rights: life, liberty, and the pursuit of happiness...."

Jefferson recognized that if the crown, the government or society is the one who gives rights, then it can also take those rights away. However, if the rights to life, liberty, and the pursuit of happiness come not from any human agency but from the Creator, then those rights can never be taken away. Therefore, the only way to have inalienable rights is if they come from the Creator himself who has made all men equal.

The Jefferson Memorial in Washington, D.C., USA

Such acknowledgement of the significance of the Creator is also found on the wall of the nearby Jefferson Memorial. It states: "Can the liberties of a nation be secure when we have removed a conviction that these liberties are the gift of God?" In promoting

16

evolution to the complete exclusion of a Creator, the National Museum of Natural History would appear to be undermining the firm basis of American liberties. When the Smithsonian Museum of Natural History teaches children that they are the result of "time, genes and a little luck,"—that they are the product of millions of years of evolution—they are removing the only firm basis for our liberties. If there is no Creator, then there can be no inalienable rights endowed by a Creator. If there is no God, then liberties cannot really be considered a gift of God.

This is a photograph of the actual words on the inside wall of the Jefferson Memorial in Washington, D.C. Several other quotes of Thomas Jefferson are also present which acknowledge the Creator.

GOD WHO GAVE US LIFE GAVE US LIBERTY. CAN THE LIBERTIES OF A NATION BE SECURE WHEN WE HAVE REMOVED A CONVICTION THAT THESE LIBERTIES ARE THE GIFT OF GOD? INDEED I TREMBLE FOR MY COUNTRY WHEN I REFLECT THAT GOD IS JUST. THAT HIS JUSTICE CANNOT SLEEP FOR-EVER. COMMERCE BETWEEN MASTER AND SLAVE IS DESPOTISM. NOTHING IS MORE CERTAINLY WRITTEN IN THE BOOK OF FATE THAN THAT THESE PEOPLE ARE TO BE FREE. ESTABLISH THE LAW FOR EDUCATING THE COMMON PEOPLE. THIS IT IS THE BUSINESS OF THE STATE TO EFFECT AND ON A GENERAL PLAN.

Although Thomas Jefferson's faith differed in some ways from the majority of evangelical Christians today, Jefferson was unswerving in his conviction that our liberties must be viewed as gifts from a Creator. It seems ironic that teachers in public schools are barred from teaching any form of creation or intelligent design because of the perceived "wall of separation"[1] that must exist between religion and the state. Such elimination of any

17

acknowledgement of creation undermines the very foundation of our freedoms in America.

Was Jefferson right?

The words on the Jefferson Memorial are a paraphrase. The full text states: "And can the liberties of a nation be thought secure when we have removed their only firm basis, a conviction in the minds of the people that these liberties are the gift of God?"[2] The full text reinforces two concepts missing from the words on the Memorial. First, the only firm basis of our liberties is that they are gifts of God. Second, this conviction must be "in the minds of the people." People must recognize the gifts of God in order to secure liberty. Jefferson raised this as a rhetorical question and we might wonder whether or not he is correct. What happens in a society that completely adopts evolution and does not acknowledge a Creator at all?

Germany serves as a good case study. Evolutionary biologist, Ernst Mayr, at the age of 100, reflected on 80 years of studying evolutionary biology, in an article in *Science*:

Curiously, I cannot pinpoint the age at which I became an evolutionist. I received all of my education in Germany, where evolution was not really controversial. In the gymnasium (equivalent to a U.S. high school), my biology teacher took evolution for granted. So, I am quite certain, did my parents-- who, to interest their three teenage sons, subscribed to a popular natural history journal that accepted evolution as a fact. Indeed, in Germany at that time there was no Protestant fundamentalism. And after I had entered university, no one raised any questions about evolution, either in my medical curriculum or in my preparations for the Ph.D. Those who were unable to adopt creation as a plausible solution for biological diversity concluded that evolution was the only rational explanation for the living world.[3]

18

Mayr describes for us the situation in Germany in the early 1900's. Evolution had been widely accepted and no one seriously questioned it. The stage was set for Hitler and the Nazi holocaust decades before it took place. Given the "fact" of evolution, if there are individuals that are more fit than others, it would stand to reason that certain races might be more fit than others.

Belief in Darwinian evolution does not automatically make one racist or a Nazi. However, Darwinian evolution is consistent with these views and can even foster them. Without a Creator, man is not made in the image of God and is instead the product of natural selection and the survival of the fittest. In his book, *From Darwin to Hitler: Evolutionary Ethics, Eugenics and Racism in Germany*, Richard Weikart argues that Darwinism played a role in the rise of eugenics, euthanasia, infanticide, abortion and racial extermination, especially in Germany. While Germany was not alone in promoting eugenics, it was promoted to the extreme there.

It is important to point out that the acceptance of evolutionary theory does not automatically engender reprehensible atrocities like the Holocaust. However, it does provide a possible foundation. Hitler and the Nazi's would not have been able to promote their aberrant views so easily without the fertile ground for their acceptance already in place. Evolutionists typically counter the charge that Darwinism paved the way for tragedies like the Holocaust with three arguments:[4]

1) Since three vastly different socio-political philosophies (Nazism, Communism, and laissez-faire capitalism) are all supposed to be based on natural selection as social Darwinism, it must be that they do not follow directly from the theory of evolution.
2) Adolf Hitler, Joseph Stalin and Andrew Carnegie based their philosophies on a misunderstanding of evolution and simply twisted it to support their own ends.
3) Even the Bible has been twisted to support excesses like witch hunts and the Crusades.

If we want to understand how such different men and different philosophies could ultimately be based on the same principles of

19

evolution, we need to identify what they have in common. In each case, man is viewed as a means to an end. There is no intrinsic value and worth derived from being created in the image of God. Therefore, although each of these philosophies comes from a different angle, the end result is the same. While it is true that the Bible has been twisted, the fact is that it was *twisted*. Social Darwinism is not a perversion of the principles of Darwinian evolution. On the contrary, it is taking them to their natural, logical conclusion. Further, if there were no connection to evolution then why is it called Social *Darwinism*? If man is the product of random chance—warmed over pond scum after a few billion years—then what difference does it make what happens? Man is but a vapor, here today and gone tomorrow and ultimately nobody cares. From such philosophies, the only thing that really matters is passing on genes to the next generation.

While we rightly recoil in disgust at the nightmare of the Holocaust, we must remember that there are modern examples of the devaluation of human life, including racism, abortion, and embryonic stem cell research. Even though there seems to be a significant difference between Nazism and embryonic stem cell research, they have a similar foundation. Both result from a failure to acknowledge human life as a sacred gift from God and denial of the special place of man, as having been created in the image of God.

Lest we think that such atrocities and poor treatment of human beings is a thing of the past, current examples highlight the persistence of the problem. Since the *Roe v Wade* decision which legalized abortion, an estimated 47 million babies have been aborted. The abortion debate has taken a modern, more pragmatic twist in regards to embryonic stem cell research and cloning. Consider this discussion between a mother and daughter which appeared in an article in the *New York Times*.[5] The mother (Harriet), whose own mother (Demetra) was suffering from Alzheimer's disease and in a nursing home, was in favor of embryonic stem cell research, while her daughter Patricia (Demetra's granddaughter) was not.

20

Harriet Spyrakos disagreed.

"You're destroying a life that hasn't started, a personality or anything," she said.

The daughter fired back, "But the embryo is a potential life."

The mother said: "It hasn't started its life. You don't know. It's only cells."

Demetra Spyrakos's granddaughter said, "It has a lot more potential life than an 80-year-old."

Such a conversation is not uncommon, and it highlights several mistaken notions prevalent in society today. First, some assume that an embryo or unborn baby does not qualify as a human life or as "a person". This rationalization is often used to support abortion. Biologically speaking, however, a fertilized egg is by definition a human life. It is alive. It is human. It cannot be anything else. The only real difference between an embryo in a dish that will be used for stem cells and an embryo in a mother's womb is real estate (location, location, location). Further, to call an embryo "only cells" ignores the fact that such a statement also applies to every human being on the planet if one takes such a reductionistic approach. A second mistaken notion is to call an embryo a "potential life" when the truth is there is no "potential" about it. Biologically speaking, there are only states: living and non-living. There is no such thing as "potentially alive". Moreover, an 80 year old is also very much alive. While a baby is expected to have a longer potential *lifespan*, the baby or embryo has no more and no less life than the 80 year old. Each of them is created in the image of God, each is a human descendant of Adam and Eve, and each possesses the God-given gift of life.

Many pregnant women are screened with serum tests and ultrasounds in order to determine if the baby they are carrying has Down syndrome. In scanning the scientific literature regarding such testing, one encounters the phrase "therapeutic abortion." It is rather ironic that any procedure that results in death would be called "therapeutic." According to a literature review from the United Kingdom, it is estimated that >90% of babies that were prenatally diagnosed with Down syndrome were terminated.[6] While similar data is not readily available for the U.S., it is likely that a significant proportion of babies diagnosed with Down syndrome or other birth defects are aborted rather than carried to term. Regardless of handicap, disability, or birth defect, every human child is precious. When certain individuals are deemed to have a "life not worthy of living," we all suffer. Yet from the standpoint of an evolutionary worldview, elimination of such "unfit" individuals is better for the human gene pool.

There are two ways to deny the uniqueness of man in creation. Thus far, we have focused on the downgrading or marring of the image of God in mankind and denying human status to human embryos. A different approach is the upgrading of other organisms to the same status as man. In spring 2006, the Spanish Socialist Party introduced a bill in the Congress of Deputies that would include apes "in the category of persons, and that they be given the moral and legal protections that currently are only enjoyed by human beings."[7] More recently, judges in Austria have been asked to grant "custody" of a chimpanzee to a British woman.[8] Enacting policies like this on a global scale is the goal of The Great Ape Project, an organization that is seeking a UN declaration that would defend the interests of apes on an equal footing with those of people. Part of the rationale for this type of action is:

> "... undeniable scientific proof that non-human great apes share more than genetically similar DNA with their human counterparts. They enjoy a rich emotional and cultural existence in which they experience emotions such as fear, anxiety and happiness. They share the intellectual capacity to create and use tools, learn and teach other languages...The Great Ape Project seeks to end the unconscionable treatment of our nearest living relatives by obtaining for non-human great apes the fundamental moral and legal protections of the right to life, the freedom from

22

arbitrary deprivation of liberty, and protection from torture." [9]

The motto on their website says "Equality beyond humanity." But why stop with apes? Why not also include dogs, pigs, cows, frogs, fish, and so on?

While this effort to extend human rights to chimpanzees, gorillas, and orangutans may seem like the work of a fringe organization, numerous well known scientists and philosophers have supported the project. From a biological perspective, there has been a push to highlight the similarity between humans and chimpanzees. Recently scientists have suggested that although chimpanzees are a different species, we should include them as a sister species in the same genus as man. [10] The underlying basis for all of this is the assumption of evolution and the idea that humans and chimpanzees share the same common ancestor instead of viewing humans as specially created in the image of God.

It would appear that Jefferson was right. Unless we acknowledge that our liberties and rights to life, liberty and the pursuit of happiness are endowed gifts of our Creator, we lose the only sure foundation for them. If there is not something that is intrinsically special about human beings, then there is no reason they should have any more value than a dog or a worm.

What is a worldview?

Worldviews are a lot like noses. Everyone has one. Even though your nose is right in front of your face, you can't see it, but you can see everyone else's. Worldviews can be very difficult to define. My daughter provided one of the most profound definitions of worldview when I asked her: "A worldview is how a person views the world." There is a certain degree of truth to this definition; however, we need something more specific. Since the way a person defines worldview is dependent on their worldview, a consensus definition of worldview will be difficult but not impossible.

23

Before the term worldview became widely used, a German word was used to mean something quite similar: *zeitgeist*. The zeitgeist referred to the spirit of the age or the intellectual, cultural and moral climate of a group of people. While the zeitgeist corresponds to the values and attitudes of a community, each individual within the group has his or her own unique perspective. The zeitgeist could rightly be described as the dominant worldview of a group of people.

A cohort, experiencing similar major life changing events will tend to respond in similar ways which are distinct from other cohorts with different experiences. For example, the Great Depression had a great impact on those growing up in the 1930's. Likewise, the Viet Nam War and Nixon's resignation greatly influenced those coming of age in the '60's and '70's. The escalating Cold War and Ronald Reagan's optimism impacted those growing up in the 1980's. More recent major influences are globalization, technological innovations such as cell phones and the internet, and 9-11 and the war on terror. While major culture shaping events tend to influence the zeitgeist, it is important to remember that the group is made up of many individuals—each having their own unique experiences that will influence their thinking. Thus, it is useful to contrast the zeitgeist of a group with the worldview of an individual.

Definitions for the term **worldview** are varied and few definitions really seem to capture everything that is meant by the term. Steve Deckard and I analyzed several different definitions of worldview and some of their strengths and weaknesses.[11] Some of the definitions are:

"A set of assumptions about how the world is and how it is organized."[12]

"...the way people think about themselves, their environments, and abstract ideas such as truth, beauty, causality, time and space."[13]

"An internal belief system about the real world—what it is, why it is and how it operates. Within a person's mind it defines the limits of what is possible and impossible."[14]

24

Some questions that are often presented as ones which help identify an individual's worldview include the following:

1) *Where did life come from?* (origins)
2) *What does it mean to be human?* (identity)
3) *What is the purpose of life?* (meaning)
4) *How should I live?* (morality)
5) *What happens after I die?* (destiny)

The answers to such questions can distinguish between the various types of worldviews, whether theism, atheism, nihilism, hedonism or others.

The focus of these definitions is the mind and lists of beliefs and assumptions. However, there seems to be much more to worldview than this. Indeed, James Sire, author of *The Universe Next Door*, argues against defining a worldview as a specific set of beliefs. Instead, he defines worldview as:

"...a commitment, a fundamental orientation of the heart, that can be expressed as a story or in a set of presuppositions (assumptions which may be true, partially true or entirely false) which we hold (consciously or subconsciously, consistently or inconsistently) about the basic constitution of reality, and that provides the foundation on which we live and move and have our being."[15]

Thus, the focus of 'worldview' should not be a specific list of beliefs but rather the orientation of the heart. This is an important distinction because often there are conflicts between what one claims to believe and what one actually does or how one behaves. It is the latter that reveals the true worldview. Moreover, unlike a specific list of beliefs, an individual's worldview is not static. A person's worldview can change throughout life depending on the experiences and personal interactions that one has. In this way, we could describe an individual's worldview as the sum total of the feelings, beliefs, memories, knowledge and experiences that are used to interpret events and make decisions. These serve as a framework for learning and a basis for behavior.

Jesus himself noted the significance of the heart. He said, "Each tree is recognized by its own fruit. People do not pick figs from thorn bushes, or grapes from briers. The good man brings good things out of the good stored up in his heart, and the evil man brings evil things out of the evil stored up in his heart. For out of the overflow of his heart his mouth speaks." (Luke 6:44-46 NIV)

What is a Biblical worldview?

The term 'Christian worldview' is used often and while it seems easy enough to understand, at the same time it is a vague concept. For example, when someone refers to the "Christian worldview" does this mean:

1) The worldview that the majority of Christians have.
2) The worldview that Christians *should* have.
3) The worldview of Christians in the early church
4) The common tenets and doctrines of Christianity

The reasons that such definitions of worldview are problematic become obvious when we consider the fact that an individual's worldview changes over time. Does a person become more (or less) Christian when their attitudes and beliefs change? Did they have a Christian worldview before? There are a number of doctrinal differences among Christians; which one is *the* Christian worldview? Unfortunately, some Christians believe in astrology or even reincarnation; do they have a Christian worldview? Clearly, a simple term like 'Christian worldview' does not have a simple meaning.

We can draw a distinction between the worldview that an individual possesses and the various categories or types of worldviews. Obviously, there are a large number of worldview categories: nihilism, humanism, communism, evolution, creation, Biblical, pagan, etc. Each of these worldviews has a set of defining beliefs or tenets. Thus, worldview types can be rigidly defined and distinguished from each other. In some cases, worldview types will be diametrically opposed. Often however, there is a spectrum of variations. While capitalism and

26

communism are considered opposites, socialism provides something in between.

In actual practice, an individual's personal worldview may be a smorgasbord of different beliefs. In politics for example, some people are socially conservative (Republican tendencies) but also fiscally liberal (Democratic tendencies), while others are the opposite. Distinguishing the worldview type from the individual's worldview is like contrasting a party platform (set of tenets) with the views of the man on the street. He or she may agree with some or even most of the beliefs but not all of them.

The more consistent the individual's worldview is, the more it will tend to be like the stereotypical worldview type. In addition, there is a need for an objective standard that can define the components of a Biblical worldview. Thus, we can define a **Biblical worldview** as the worldview that is based on and derived from both the Old and New Testaments of the Bible. In this way, the Scripture itself sets the standard. Where two biblical concepts or principles appear to conflict, other passages can be used to shed light on the subject. Thus, Scripture is used to interpret Scripture.

In proposing such a Biblical worldview as a standard, we should consider what the Bible says about worldviews. Although the term "worldview" is not found anywhere in the Bible, the concept is mentioned in several different passages throughout:

"Do not conform any longer to the pattern of this world, but be transformed by the renewing of your mind. Then you will be able to test and approve what God's will is—his good, pleasing and perfect will." Romans 12:2 (NIV)

"Finally, brothers, whatever is true, whatever is noble, whatever is right, whatever is pure, whatever is lovely, whatever is admirable—if anything is excellent or praiseworthy—think about such things." Philippians 4:8 (NIV)

"We demolish arguments and every pretension that sets itself up against the knowledge of God, and we take captive every thought to make it obedient to Christ." 2 Corinthians 10:5 (NIV)

"See to it that no one takes you captive through hollow and deceptive philosophy, which depends on human tradition and the basic principles of this world rather than on Christ." Colossians 2:8 (NIV)

These and other verses help us to understand our worldview from a Biblical perspective. Perhaps the key benefit to having a Biblical worldview is shown in Romans 12:2. If our thinking is consistent with the Bible, then we can better discern God's will. **The more our commitments and the orientation of our heart are in line with Scripture, the closer our individual worldview will be in line with God's heart.** As our thinking and behavior conform to Scripture, then we will increasingly have 'the mind of Christ.' In contrast, if our thinking and behavior are out of sync with what the Bible teaches, then we might be described as "double-minded." In Scripture, James admonishes us to make sure our beliefs and behavior coincide: "Do not merely listen to the word and so deceive yourselves. Do what it says." James 1:22 (NIV)

Origins and worldview thinking

While there may be many separate components to an individual's worldview, the most foundational aspect is origins. This is because the answer to the question "*Where did life come from?*" actually helps shape the answers to all of the other questions related to worldview. Another way to ask the origins question is: *Is there a creator or not (and if so, who or what)?* Notice how the answer to this question impacts the answers to other worldview questions. If there is no creator, then there can be no plan or purpose to the universe. The concepts of value and meaning in human life become nonsensical, and human life becomes focused on little more than pleasure. "How should I live?" becomes totalitarian or anarchist, and "what happens after we die?" is meaningless. The Jesuit theologian and historian, Henri de Lubac, noted the consequences of atheism. "It is not true, as is sometimes said, that man cannot organize the world without God. What is true is that, without God, he can only organize it against man."[16]

28

In a consistent Biblical, creationist worldview, we find answers to the worldview questions like this:

> *1. Where did life come from?*
> Life was specially created by the God of the Bible.
> *2. What does it mean to be human?*
> Man was created by God specially and separately from all of the other creatures. Man is uniquely created in the image of God.
> *3. What is the purpose of life?*
> The purpose of life is to give glory and honor to God.
> *4. How should we live?*
> People should love the Lord with all their heart, soul, strength and mind and their neighbor as themselves.
> *5. What happens after I die?*
> Those who have been redeemed through faith in Jesus Christ and his resurrection will go to be with the Lord, while those who have not go to eternal punishment.

Without the acknowledgement of God as the Creator at the start, there would be no basis for the answers to the other questions. Further, if a person believes the creator is Allah, space aliens or some other god, then that will impact on the answers to the other worldview questions. It doesn't work the other way around. You cannot begin with the answers to questions 2-4 and work backwards to get the answer to question 1. The origins issue serves as the foundation and glue to a person's worldview.

Conclusion

What difference does a worldview make? It makes all the difference. This chapter began with a quote from *Alice in Wonderland.* Since Alice said she didn't care where she ended up, the Cheshire Cat answered that it didn't matter which way she went. In a similar way, if we don't know or care about how we came to be, then why should it matter where we end up after we die or how we get there?

After going through the National Museum of Natural History, I couldn't help but be reminded of the words of Paul in Romans 1:

> "The wrath of God is being revealed from heaven against all the godlessness and wickedness of men who suppress the truth by their wickedness, since what may be known about God is plain to them, because God has made it plain to them. For since the creation of the world God's invisible qualities—his eternal power and divine nature—have been clearly seen, being understood from what has been made, so that men are without excuse.
> "For although they knew God, they neither glorified him as God nor gave thanks to him, but their thinking became futile and their foolish hearts were darkened. Although they claimed to be wise, they became fools and exchanged the glory of the immortal God for images made to look like mortal man and birds and animals and reptiles."
> Romans 1:18-23 (NIV)

Therefore, what may be known about God is plain through His creative power. Yet, it is this clear, plain truth that is suppressed by the theory of evolution. What happens because of that? When people fail to acknowledge God as Creator and do not glorify Him as such, they give up a lot. They exchange the glory of being created in the image of God for being the descendents of cavemen, monkeys, reptiles and worms.

---

[1] The often used reference to the "wall of separation" actually comes from a letter that Jefferson wrote to the Danbury Baptists in 1802. In the letter, Jefferson also wrote in this letter: "I reciprocate your kind prayers for the protection & blessing of the common father and creator of man..." The full text can be read from the Library of Congress at: http://www.loc.gov/loc/lcib/9806/danpost.html

[2] Jefferson, T. 1794. THOMAS JEFFERSON, NOTES ON THE STATE OF VIRGINIA, QUERY XVIII.

[3] Mayr, Ernst. 2004. "80 years of Watching the Evolutionary Scenery" *Science* **305**:46-47.

[4] Thwaites, William "Would We All Behave Like Animals? A Conversation" www.ncseweb.org downloaded April 8, 2006.

30

[5] Fountain, John W "President's Decision Does Not End the Debate" The New York Times, August 12, 2001

[6] Mansfield, C., Hopfer, S., and Marteau, T.M. 1999. Termination rates after prenatal diagnosis of Down syndrome, spina bifida, anencephaly, and Turner and Klinefelter syndromes: a systematic literature review. *Prenatal Diagnosis* **19**(9): 808-812

[7] "Socialists: Give apes human rights", The Spain Herald Libertad Digital http://www.spainherald.com/3438.html downloaded April 30, 2006

[8] Geoghegan, Tom. 2007. "Should apes have human rights?" http://news.bbc.co.uk/1/hi/magazine/6505691.stm

[9] www.greatapeproject.org Downloaded March 31, 2007

[10] Wildman, D.E., Uddin, M., Liu, G., Grossman, L.I. and Goodman, M. 2003. Implications of natural selection in shaping 99.4% nonsynonymous DNA identity between humans and chimpanzees: Enlarging genus *Homo*, *Proc. Natl. Acad. Sci. USA* **100**(12):7181-7188.

[11] Deckard, Steve. and DeWitt, David A. 2003. *Developing a Creator-Centered Worldview* Vision Publishing, Ramona, California p. 87-90.

[12] Luker, K. 1984. *Abortion and the politics of motherhood.* Berkeley: University of California Press page 193 as quoted in: Emerson, M. 1996. Through tinted glasses: Religion, worldviews, and abortion attitudes. *J. Scientific Study Religion* **35**(1): 41-45.

[13] Allen, N., Crawley, F. 1998. Voices form the bridge: Worldview conflicts of Kickapoo students of Science. *Journal of Research in Science Teaching* **35**:111-132

[14] Wisniewski, M.E. 1994. The Worldview approach to critical thinking, *Proceedings of the Third International Conference on Creationism*, 593-607 page 596.

[15] Sire, James W. 2004. *Naming the Elephant* Intervarsity Press page 161.

[16] de Lubac, Henri. 1995. *The Drama of Atheistic Humanism* Ignatius Press.

2

A Different Kind of Science

"Our theory of evolution has become...one which cannot be refuted by any possible observation. Every conceivable observation can be fitted into it. It is thus 'outside of empirical science' but not necessarily false. No one can think of ways in which to test it. Ideas, either without basis or based on a few laboratory experiments carried out in extremely simplified systems, have attained currency far beyond their validity. They have become part of an evolutionary dogma accepted by most of us as part of our training."

P. Ehrlich and L.C. Birch[1]

What is science?

A common definition of science is *science is a way of knowing*. Science is an approach; it is a method for finding information about reality, about how things work or of what they are made. Our scientific investigations have led to significant human accomplishments including landing a man on the moon and deciphering the human genetic code. However, science is not the only way of knowing or discerning truth. Indeed, there are other ways that we can know things besides using the scientific method. For example, if I want to know whether my wife loves me or not, I do not use the scientific method! I listen to the words that she says, "I love you" and I see the confirmation in her actions. In the same way, to know that God exists and that he loves each person, we cannot use the scientific method. Instead, we must look to Scripture and God's action in the world and believe. Good and evil, right and wrong are also not discernable through the scientific method. So, while science can tell us a great deal about the world we live in, it cannot tell us everything.

Many modern scientists have attempted to define science in strictly naturalistic terms. They say that science is the process of seeking naturalistic explanations for phenomena. **Naturalism** is a belief system that contends that 'nature' is all there is and denies the supernatural and miracles altogether. On the one hand, this seems reasonable because we cannot apply the scientific method to God's activity. However, this definition also implies that *only* naturalistic explanations should be considered by reasonable, educated people.

An example of the naturalistic assumptions implicit in science comes from a letter about intelligent design to the prestigious science journal *Nature*. Dr Scott Todd from Kansas State University wrote:

> "Even if all the data point to an intelligent designer, such an hypothesis is excluded from science because it is not naturalistic."[2]

Such a statement is inconsistent with science being defined as an open-minded, objective search for truth. It reveals instead the naturalistic bias that dominates modern science.

A closer examination of this naturalistic assumption reveals an inconsistency. If the spiritual dimension is beyond the scope of scientific investigation, how can scientific investigation demonstrate that the spiritual dimension does not exist? Scientists often assert that evolution is an unguided process. But how can anyone use the scientific method to *demonstrate* that evolution is unguided? The fact is that it cannot be done. Moreover, the scientific method cannot be used to show that mutations are random either. Thus, evolutionary scientists assume that evolution is an unguided, random process without the ability to test and affirm this assumption. This sounds like faith to me.

34

While I perform experiments in my laboratory, I do not expect a miracle to keep cells alive after they are treated with a toxic compound. However, I expect a particular drug to counter the affects of the toxin. When I do so, I am looking for a natural explanation and mechanism for the action of the drug. At the same time, I pray to the Lord for wisdom, that he will help me to understand the results and grant me success from my labors. These are not inconsistent. God has ordained the universe to obey certain regular natural laws. At the same time, there is a spiritual dimension and God occasionally intervenes with miracles.

This is a picture of me in my laboratory I am looking at cells using a fluorescent microscope.[3]

Generations of scientists have been taught to equate religion and faith with superstition and the "Dark Ages." At the same time, science is defined as a noble, objective enterprise and a triumph of reason over superstition and faith. Religion is thus compartmentalized into irrelevance, humbled into subservience to science or described as a characteristic of primitive stages of culture. However, such a view ignores the significant contributions of many scientists of the past who were motivated by their view of God. Kepler, Newton, Faraday, and many others believed in a Creator. Their belief in God led them to expect order in the universe. They approached science and the world with a wonder and awe as they saw the wisdom of God manifested in nature. Their faith and belief in the supernatural did not prevent them from studying nature and making great scientific discoveries. In fact, the opposite is true. They believed in a Creator who made

35

the universe orderly and this provided a motivation to explore and uncover the wisdom with which God had made everything.

How science really works

Many people receive their first dose of "real science" when preparing for a science fair in middle or high school. Such a setting is where many of us learn what the term *hypothesis* means and how experiments work. Although nearly all of these projects are elementary compared to the work done by professional scientists, science fair projects help students to learn about the process of doing science.

Science begins by observation, examining the world and the way it works. The scientist identifies a problem or asks a question: How does it work? Why does it work? What is it made out of? To answer the question, the scientist proposes a **hypothesis**, a testable explanation or solution to the problem. A good hypothesis is one that is testable, there is an experiment or test that can be performed which could potentially demonstrate that the hypothesis is wrong. Thus, *experiments* and *testability* are key characteristics of scientific investigation.

A hypothesis which correctly explains phenomena will stand up to repeated testing from a variety of angles. If a hypothesis is inconsistent with experimental observations, then the hypothesis needs to be modified or discarded altogether. Experiments must be repeated in order to have any value. Thus, repeatability in time and place is necessary for scientific studies to be published. Scientists are expected to perform experiments many times to make sure that their results are consistent before publishing the work.

This is the ideal way that science operates. In reality, scientists typically spend huge amounts of time trying to get and maintain research funding. Thus, hypothesis driven research tends to focus on what can get funding. In addition, science is a human enterprise. As such, personalities and prestige often play a larger role than they should. Prominent scientists can lead "research fads" that other scientists just follow. The research fad works much the way that fashion trends follow Hollywood celebrities.

After awhile, the trendsetters get on another hot research topic, and the previous topic goes the way of last year's hemline. Top researchers are greeted and treated like the scientific equivalent of rock stars. Science is a competitive business and researchers often long for patents or an article in *Nature* or *Science* (the science equivalent of getting a "star" on Hollywood Blvd.) The grand prize in science is the Nobel Prize which is similar to winning an Academy Award or Golden Globe. Although this comparison of the scientific enterprise to Hollywood is somewhat cynical, it highlights the fact that scientists are people too. They are driven by and blinded by the same passions that everyone else is. Getting a Ph.D. and a white lab coat with your name on it does not somehow make the scientist super-human.

Also in middle school science classes, students often develop a mistaken understanding of the distinctions between scientific hypotheses, theories and laws. We come away with the notion that if hypotheses are really good and stand up to enough tests they can be advanced to theories. Then theories which are really, really good can be advanced to laws. In reality, there is no such progression because we are dealing with three different things. As noted above, a **hypothesis** is a testable explanation for a specific phenomenon. A **theory** is best defined as a set of related hypotheses that are bound together to describe a phenomenon. Theories cannot be proven, but they can be refuted by new observations. Usually theories will be modified to accommodate the new data. A scientific **law** is a generalized statement about an aspect of nature and is universally confirmed. Scientific laws are considered certain and can often be reduced to a mathematical formula.

Thus, we can distinguish between the Law of Gravity and the Theory of Gravity and a hypothesis about gravity. The Law of Gravity states that two bodies exert an attractive force in proportion to the product of the masses and inversely proportional to the square of the distance between them. Or, put more simply, what goes up must come down! The Law of gravity can be expressed by the formula[*]:

$$F = G\frac{m_1 m_2}{r^2}$$

This formula has been demonstrated to work consistently regardless of whether we are looking at basketballs and the earth or the moon and the earth or even the planets and the sun. In contrast, the Theory of Gravity describes how and why gravity is supposed to work. It involves many components, facts, observations, and assumptions including the curvature of space, relativity, presumed expansion of the universe and more. An example of a hypothesis about gravity was that light coming from stars would be bent by the gravity of the sun. Such a hypothesis was indeed confirmed by observation in 1919. While hypotheses, theories and laws all make up our knowledge and understanding about the natural world, all three of them represent different aspects of that knowledge.

Empirical Vs. Historical Sciences

When most people think about science, they think about biology, chemistry and physics. They think about technological and medical advancements, the scientific method and experiments. These areas of science are called operational sciences or empirical sciences. Knowledge gained from these areas relies heavily on the scientific method and testing hypotheses. Scientists use their five senses (or extensions using equipment such as microscopes and telescopes) in the present. Experiments are repeated and modified numerous times in order to replicate studies. But there is another type of science, namely historical science.

Historical sciences answer different questions from empirical sciences and take a very different approach. Historical sciences include archeology, geology, forensics and other disciplines that work to explain past events. Whereas empirical sciences test one

---

[*] F = Force due to gravity, G is the gravitational constant, m_1 and m_2 are the masses of the two objects, r is the distance between them.

38

hypothesis at a time with an experiment, historical sciences make use of multiple competing hypotheses. These represent a variety of different explanations that "compete" with each other as the best one. Each hypothesis serves as a framework for interpreting data. Since questions of a historical nature address singular events in the past, it is impossible to repeat them. No experiments can be done today to test them in the same way that empirical sciences are tested.

Different Types of Questions

Empirical Sciences
What is it?
Why does it happen?
How does it work?
Can we change it?

Historical Sciences
What happened?
Why did it happen?
How did it come to be?
What/Who did it?
When did it happen?

Consider the investigation of a crime scene. Forensic scientists want to determine how and when a particular crime took place. In the case of a death, they may need to determine whether an accident took place or whether there was foul play. (Was it chance or intelligent design?) The investigators obviously cannot repeat the crime, and so empirical science does not apply. Although the investigators may try to simulate portions of the crime (such as firing a bullet from a suspect's gun), in reality, it cannot be repeated in every detail. They may begin with many suspects (multiple competing hypotheses) and slowly work to eliminate them. If they are fortunate, there may be an eyewitness that can provide testimony. Eye witness testimony is invaluable for solving a crime or other historical question. The person who was there knows the truth, what actually happened. In the absence of such testimony, the investigators must carry out the arduous task of ruling out suspect after suspect until only one remains.

Let's contrast empirical and historical sciences again. In empirical science, we might formulate a hypothesis that a particular molecule is toxic to bacteria. We can perform an experiment where we administer the molecule to bacteria and determine whether they die. If so, we can repeat it several times

39

with different concentrations of the molecule and different types of bacteria. With the use of a control,[4] we can demonstrate that the molecule in question alone is responsible for death of the bacteria.

In the case of a historical question, we may observe a toxic compound in the blood of a person who has died. Before concluding that the toxin killed the person, we would first have to rule out other possible causes of death. For example, a slow acting toxin in a person who drowned would have been killed by the water and not the toxin. After eliminating other causes of death, many questions remain. Was this an accident? Was this a suicide? If this was a murder, then who did it and why? We can make hypotheses as to the suspect and motive, but we cannot do experiments in the same way as occurs for empirical research. To solve the crime, the investigator must consider multiple suspects with multiple motives—each representing a working hypothesis.

When using multiple competing hypotheses, a key feature is **robustness**. A theory or hypothesis that is robust is one that accommodates the most data from all observations. A robust theory makes sense and has the least amount of conflict. For example, a suspect that has an alibi or was out of town would be ruled out as a possibility. Suspects with no motive might also be ruled out. The strongest suspect would have motive, opportunity, and lack an alibi. DNA or other corroborating evidence would contribute to the robustness, or case against the individual. However, without eye witness testimony, even with robust evidence, there may not be enough evidence to convict the suspect. This happens whenever there is reasonable doubt. Sometimes, alternatives cannot be ruled out completely and thus there may still be some other explanation for what happened in the past.

Scientists use mental constructs or frameworks as models to explain and interpret data. Often, an object or process cannot be directly observed and so the model serves as a substitute. Alternatively, there may be some evidence that supports the accuracy of a model, but no experiment can be done to test it directly. Therefore, models are tentative explanations for phenomena. A scientific model is very much like a theory and in some ways can be used interchangeably. Models can be used to make predictions that can be tested using the scientific method but

40

the model itself cannot be proven. Hypotheses that are confirmed will contribute to the robustness of the model. Therefore, the more observations that are consistent with the model, the more the model is considered to reflect reality.

Now, when evolution is referred to as a theory, this does not mean that it is just a guess or a hunch. The theory of evolution refers to the proposed model of how new species arise and change over time through an unbroken chain of common ancestors. From within the evolution model, observations can be made that will be consistent or inconsistent with the theory. There are certain rules and assumptions that comprise the theory and establish the bounds of data interpretation. In the same way, we could also consider a "theory of creation" which would be a model to describe origins from a creation perspective. This model would involve different rules and assumptions which would establish the bounds of data interpretation. Evolution and creation can both be defined as models to address historical questions. Thus, they are alternative approaches or frameworks to explain origins.

Creation vs. Evolution Assumptions

Creation	Evolution
God is the Creator	There is no significant role for God
Direct acts of God	Natural law & Processes only
Young age for earth	Very old earth & universe
Scripture is inerrant	Scientific method only source
Bible is source of truth	for truth

Questions related to origins cannot be answered or tested by experimental methods in the same way that many questions in biochemistry or cell biology can be. Observations and inferences are interpreted within the model framework and will either support the model or not. Ernst Mayr (1904-2005), who was one of the leading evolutionists in the world, wrote:

"Evolution is a historical process that cannot be proven by the same arguments and methods by which purely physical

41

or functional phenomena can be documented. Evolution as a whole, and the explanation of particular evolutionary events, must be inferred from observations. Such inferences subsequently must be tested again and again against new observation, and the original inference is either falsified or considerably strengthened when confirmed by all of these tests. However, most inferences made by evolutionists have by now been tested successfully so often that they are accepted as certainties."[5]

Now when he says that inferences are "tested again and again against new observation" this does not mean that there is actually any experimental test done to confirm it. The inferences are being compared with other inferences derived with different methods but similar assumptions. Just because someone can come to the same conclusion several times does not make an inference valid. There may be more reasons to accept the inference, but it remains an inference.

Evolutionists themselves will agree with the distinction that evolution is a historical rather than empirical science as noted by Mayr above. However, they typically blur this distinction. When people claim that teaching creation in science class would be "the end of science" or that other countries will advance much further than us because they teach evolution, they are confusing empirical and historical science. Does a computer work differently if the person who designed it was a creationist? How about a rocket or a bridge? Does the MRI (Magnetic Resonance Imaging) system function worse because the inventor, Dr. Raymond Damadian happens to be a creationist? Obviously, the origins beliefs of a scientist do not prevent them from doing empirical science research. Likewise students who believe in creation or are taught about *both* creation and evolution can still make good scientists.

A matter of faith

A creationist explanation for origins is not only appropriate, but also exists on equal footing with the evolutionist explanation regarding matters of history. Neither explanation can be

42

experimentally tested or subjected to the scientific method. Both of them begin with certain assumptions and both establish rules about what counts as data and the interpretations that are allowed. The creationist explanation for origins uses the Bible as providing data (eye witness testimony in fact) whereas the Bible is excluded from an evolutionist perspective. The starting assumptions that are made under each theory will play a decisive role in shaping the discussion and the final conclusions. Ultimately, neither model can be proven. Both must be accepted by faith.

We should not underestimate the role of the heart in how a person approaches questions related to origins. In many cases, it is not a matter of evidence at all. For example, for some people who reject creation, no amount of evidence to the contrary will make a difference. Consider the Pharisees at the time of Jesus. They had more evidence that Jesus Christ was the Son of God than we could ever hope to have. They saw him, talked with him, and had their questions answered. They saw the miracles. They saw him die on the cross and watched as he was buried in the tomb. They even asked to have a guard posted and the tomb sealed in case the disciples tried to do something. But when they found the tomb empty, they did not worship Christ but instead made up the story that the disciples stole the body. Thus, for some, no matter how much evidence for creation mounts up, they will reject it outright.

The Bible does not argue for God's existence nor does it offer "proof" of creation. In fact, both are assumed: "In the beginning, God..." Nonetheless, there is plain evidence to support both for those who have open eyes. Romans 1:20 says: "For since the creation of the world God's invisible qualities--his eternal power and divine nature--have been clearly seen, being understood from what has been made, so that men are without excuse." In other words, we can find evidence for God in what he made. This evidence is so overwhelming that one has to deliberately ignore it in order to deny it. But it does take faith.

We often hear a distorted definition of faith. Some make comments about the "blind faith" of creationists or they contend that creationists believe in spite of the alleged "overwhelming evidence" for evolution. However, Christianity is a reasoned faith and there are good reasons for the doctrines that we hold dear—

43

including creation. The Bible does not teach the believer to "check his or her mind at the door." Quite the opposite, in Isaiah 1:18, the Lord says, "Come now, let us reason together...." And in Matthew 22:37, it says: "Love the Lord your God with all your heart, and with all your soul and all your *mind.*"

Having faith in God is not intellectual suicide and neither is it a crutch for the weak minded. Hebrews 11 gives us a good Biblical definition of what faith is:

"Now faith is being sure of what we hope for and certain of what we do not see." Hebrews 11:1 (NIV)

"By faith we understand that the universe was formed at God's command, so that what is seen was not made out of what was visible." Hebrews 11:3 (NIV)

"And without faith it is impossible to please God, because anyone who comes to him must believe that he exists and that he rewards those who earnestly seek him." Hebrews 11:6 (NIV)

In this context, then, faith is not going *against* the evidence but just a little beyond it. All it takes is faith the size of a mustard seed to believe that God exists and the eyes can see the wonder of creation.

When creation is defined as religion and evolution is defined as science, they are placed on an unfair playing field. Ultimately, both creation and evolution are belief systems. We have already discussed how creation science can function as a historical science and acknowledged the faith involved. Evolution, although based on naturalism, requires faith also. Evolutionists go "just a little beyond the evidence" to justify their conclusions, however they go in the direction of naturalism. Thus, it is faith. Richard Lewontin explains:

'We take the side of science *in spite* of the patent absurdity of some of its constructs, *in spite* of its failure to fulfill many of its extravagant promises of health and life, *in spite* of the

44

tolerance of the scientific community for unsubstantiated just-so stories, because we have a prior commitment, a commitment to materialism. It is not that the methods and institutions of science somehow compel us to accept a material explanation of the phenomenal world, but, on the contrary, that we are forced by our a priori adherence to material causes to create an apparatus of investigation and a set of concepts that produce material explanations, no matter how counter-intuitive, no matter how mystifying to the uninitiated. Moreover, that materialism is an absolute, for we cannot allow a Divine Foot in the door.'[6]

Thus, the evolutionist too has a belief system—a belief system based on material causes which excludes the possibility of the divine. When evolutionists insist that they alone are scientific because they look at evidence rather than faith, it is only because they ignore their foundational assumption of naturalism. Naturalism is an assumption that cannot be proven.

A different kind of science

Origins science is very much a historical science. Not one of us was there to observe what happened in the past. Therefore, we are left with multiple competing hypotheses to explain the data from the natural world. Did the origin of life happen through natural laws and processes alone or was it the result of a Divine Creator? We can make two competing hypotheses:

1) Life came about as non-living chemicals came together and gave rise to the first living thing that evolved into everything else. (Evolution model)
2) God made living things and called them to reproduce after their kind. (Creation model)

Since the scientific method cannot rule out the possibility of a Creator, we should not exclude creation as an explanation for origins. Thus, we are left with two mutually exclusive competing hypotheses. In order to determine which one is correct, we will

45

consider the robustness of each. Which one accommodates the most data and support from observations? Which one is the most consistent with what we see in the world? Which one has the least complications or problems?

Creation science is a different kind of science, but it is still science. The creationist is not looking for miracles around every corner, but acknowledges one of God's greatest miracles—creation. I teach undergraduate biochemistry and cell biology. Sometimes when I teach about aspects of life such as metabolism or the cell division cycle I am awestruck by the wisdom of the God who spoke it into existence. At such times, I am moved to worship and am honored to share such moments with the students in my class. In contrast, to teach such amazing beauty and complexity while attributing it only to "random chance", mutation, and luck seems very hollow. Approaching science from a creationist perspective can be very fulfilling as the scientist can revel in the wisdom and glory of the Creator.

---

[1] Birch, L.C. and Ehrlich, P.R. 1967. Evolutionary history and population biology. *Nature* **214**: 349-352

[2] Todd, S.C. 1999. A view from Kansas on that evolution debate. *Nature* **401**(6752):423

[3] This photograph was taken by Les Schofer.

[4] An experimental control is a duplicate sample that has not been perturbed in any way. For example, to test the effectiveness of a drug, a placebo is used as a control to eliminate alternative explanations besides the drug.

[5] Mayr, Ernst, 2001. *What evolution is* Basic Books. New York ISBN 0-465-04426-3 page 13

[6] Richard Lewontin, 1997. Billions and billions of demons, *The New York Review*, p. 31, 9 January 1997.

3

A Day is a Day

"For me, there really is no conflict here—if God chose to use the mechanism of evolution to create creatures in his image, who are we to say that's not how we would have done it"[1]

--Francis S. Collins, Director
National Human Genome Research Institute

"The LORD God formed the man from the dust of the ground and breathed into his nostrils the breath of life, and the man became a living being."

Genesis 2:7 (NIV)

The Bible does not set out to prove the existence of God nor does it provide arguments and evidence to prove that God created the heavens and the earth. These are assumed. Indeed, the entire Bible is written without the tiniest shred of doubt regarding this fact. From the very first verse, Genesis 1:1: "In the beginning God created the heavens and the earth." (NIV) God is there *before* the beginning. He is before heaven and before the earth.

It may be surprising, but there is a verse in Scripture that chronologically precedes Genesis 1:1 and that is John 1:1-2: "In the beginning was the Word, and the Word was with God and the Word was God. He was with God in the beginning." (NIV) The reason this verse is chronologically before Genesis 1:1 is because it is describing the fellowship between the Father and the Son before there was a heaven and an earth. No attempt is made to prove this fact either. It is also assumed.

Several verses in Scripture support the premise that the Son of God was with the Father before the formation of the heavens and the earth and that He was involved in the process:

> "Through him (the Word) all things were made; without him nothing was made that has been made." John 1:3 (NIV)

> "He is the image of the invisible God, the firstborn over all creation. For by him all things were created: things in heaven and on earth, visible and invisible, whether thrones or powers or rulers or authorities; all things were created by him and for him. He is before all things, and in him all things hold together." Colossians 1:15-17 (NIV)

> "'And now, Father, glorify me in your presence with the glory I had with you before the world began.'" John 17:5 (NIV)

Additionally, as we see in many of the miracles that Jesus performed in his earthly ministry, he had a unique control over everything in the world. Not only was Jesus able to heal people of a wide variety of ailments, but he turned water into wine, walked on water, multiplied the fishes and loaves and raised the dead. Notice the response of the disciples when Jesus calmed the storm: "Who is this? Even the wind and the waves obey him!" Mark 4:41 (NIV) The reason that the wind and waves obeyed him is because *he* created them. Interestingly, in John 1:1 Christ is called the *Word* of God and throughout the process of creation God *said*...and it was so. Thus, all things were made by and through the Word of God.

Much of the dispute regarding origins is over how much of it was supernatural and how much was done by natural laws and processes—whether ordained by God or not. One way to answer the question is to consider the miracles of Jesus and how they might be similar to creation. Several of Jesus' miracles were

48

performed by **fiat** and *ex nihilo*. This means by his command, from nothing. For example, when the fishes and loaves were multiplied, the extra bread and fish came from nothing. This is a clear violation of the laws of thermodynamics as everything in nature tells us that matter does not come into existence from nothing. In addition, when Jesus changed the water into wine, although there was water in the jars, the wine came from nowhere. If you saw it and tasted it, you could not tell it from wine that had been around for quite some time. Indeed, unless you were one of the men who filled the jars with water, you would never know.

The Bible describes creation as occurring at God's command from nothing. This is clearly spelled out in Hebrews 11:3: "By faith we understand that the universe was formed at God's *command*, so that what is seen was not made out of what was visible." (NIV) Our understanding of this is that by the power of God's word *alone*, all of the matter and energy in the universe simply *appeared*. Of course this is an assumption, a statement of belief which cannot be proven. It is *by faith*. In contrast, if a person rejects this view and does not believe that God created the universe then they also do so *by faith* as the opposite cannot be proven either. The miracles of Jesus Christ parallel the miracles of creation. Thus, if we believe the miracles that Jesus Christ performed, it is no stretch to believe creation occurred in the same way—at God's command from nothing. In contrast, if we believe the miracles of Jesus, but then deny the miracles of creation, we are inconsistent.

Obviously, our redemption by grace through faith in Christ Jesus is reason for us to praise God. But the whole of creation—angels, animals, plants, rocks, stars, planets, you, me—everything gives praise for creation. God is praised for remembering his people, but over and over one of the chief reasons for praise to the Lord is for creation. Consider the following verses:

"Let them praise the name of the LORD for he commanded and they were *created*." Psalm 148:5 (NIV)

"The heavens are yours, and also the earth; you founded the world and all that is in it." Psalm 89:11 (NIV)

49

"Worship the LORD with gladness; come before him with joyful songs. Know that the LORD is GOD. It is he who made us and we are his." Psalm 100:2-3 (NIV)

"How many are your works, O LORD! In wisdom you made them all; the earth is full of your creatures. Psalm 104:24 (NIV)

"You are worthy, our LORD and God, to receive glory and honor and power, for you created all things and by your will they were created and have their being." Rev 4:11 (NIV)

While humanity, as created in the image of God, gives praise to our Creator and Redeemer, the rest of creation praises God as their Creator only.

Biblical (Young Earth) Creation

Before discussing the variety of origins views that people subscribe to, it will be useful to present some of the basic points of Biblical creation. Besides the question of "Who?" there are two other questions that are widely discussed regarding origins: "How?", and "How long?" From a young earth creation perspective, these questions are answered: by the Word of God in six normal days roughly 6,000 years ago.

According to Biblical creation, Genesis 1-11 provides an accurate, historical account of real events that occurred as recorded. The creation of the heavens and the earth took six days and took place in the exact order that is specified. On each day, a normal solar day ~24 hours in length, God made different things and then rested on the seventh day. Adam and Eve were real people just like us. The Fall in the Garden of Eden was an actual event that could have been video recorded if the technology were available. There was no animal death prior to the Fall. Noah's Flood covered the entire globe from pole to pole and destroyed everything that lived on dry land except those individuals that were with Noah on the ark. Following the flood, God confused the

50

languages of people and caused them to disperse around the world from the Tower of Babel. Thus, Biblical creation takes a straightforward approach to the text of Genesis.

There are two separate issues regarding the age of the earth. The first is the length of the days, whether they represent true days or long periods of time. The second issue is how long ago the creation took place. As indicated, Biblical creation holds ~6,000 years for the age of the earth. This date is obtained by adding the ages of the people that are listed in the genealogies Genesis 5 and 11. This provides a continuous genealogy from Adam to Abraham. From Abraham to the Exodus from Egypt, and then from the Exodus to the time of King David provides the rest of the timeline.

The young earth creation perspective has been held by Christians throughout the centuries. Martin Luther expounded on this topic in his commentary on Genesis:

"We know from Moses that the world was not in existence before 6,000 years ago."[2]

"...he (Moses) calls 'a spade a spade,' i.e. he employs the terms 'day and 'evening' without allegory, just as we customarily do."[3]

"Therefore...we assert that Moses spoke in the literal sense, not allegorically or figuratively, i.e., that the world with all of its creatures, was created within six days, as the words read. If we do not comprehend the reason for this, let us remain pupils and leave the job of teacher to the Holy Spirit.[4]

Surprisingly, at the time of Luther, one of the challenges to Genesis that he had to face was the fact that people couldn't believe it took *so long as* six days for God to make the heavens and the earth. Some preferred to compress that time into one day or an instant. Luther challenged such views by the plain words of the text.

51

Perhaps one of the most maligned young earth creationists is Archbishop James Ussher. Ussher was a famous and respected historian of his day. He wrote a history of the world from the beginning of creation through the fall of Jerusalem. It was called *The Annals of the World*. A current English translation of the book is over 860 pages long and it covers all of this ancient history in amazing detail.

The reason that this scholar has been criticized so much is probably because of his claim that Day 1 of creation took place on the evening preceding Oct 23 in 4004 B.C.[5] Because this day seems so random, it implies that Ussher didn't know what he was talking about and couldn't possibly be right. However, a closer examination of this date reveals that it is not quite so random. This day represents the first Sunday after the autumnal equinox. October 23 from the Julian calendar corresponds to September 21 on the Gregorian calendar (the one we currently use).

Ussher developed his chronology assuming that the ages listed for the people in the genealogy were accurate and that there were none missing. This gave the year of 4004 B.C. That seems reasonable enough, but why would anyone pick the Oct 23rd date?

The selection of the date makes more sense when we understand the rationale and its relationship to the Jewish calendar. The Jewish people started their week on Sunday and their days began at sundown. Therefore, it would be a reasonable assumption that the beginning of creation would be on the evening before a Sunday. This would make the seventh day a Saturday which Jews recognize as the Sabbath. Importantly, October 23 would have been the date of the Jewish New Year (**Rosh Hashanah**) in 4004 B.C. So if you are going to pick a day in the year that would be Day 1, the date of the Jewish New Year is probably the most reasonable one to choose. So this date is not quite as arbitrary as we might expect.

Besides suggesting the date for creation, Ussher also posited that the Fall took place on the tenth day. While we might anticipate that the Fall would have happened relatively soon (as it must have happened before Adam and Eve conceived any children) the tenth day also seems arbitrary at first glance. However, this corresponds to **Yom Kippur** which is the Day of

52

Atonement. This is a day set aside for prayer and fasting. It is the holiest day in Judaism and was the day for offering the scapegoats (Leviticus 16:8-10). Ussher believed that this was the day of the Fall and the day that God clothed Adam & Eve with animal skins to cover their nakedness.

Whether or not creation and the Fall actually took place on those exact dates we cannot be sure. However, the choice of the Jewish New Year and the Day of Atonement demonstrate careful consideration. Moreover, the choice of 4004 B.C. is a good approximation as the genealogies in Genesis give a continuous record. (This will be discussed more in Chapter 6.)

Rather than providing arguments and support for the young earth creation position, I will discuss several origins compromises. In contrasting these to young earth creation and pointing out their flaws, the supporting evidence for Biblical creation will become clear through the objections and rebuttals of the compromise positions. We will begin by looking at two views that take a completely non-literal approach to Genesis 1-11 and the timeframes involved (Theistic evolution and Framework Hypothesis). Then, we will consider views that take certain portions of Genesis 1-11 as real history while rejecting others (Gap Theory and Day Age/Progressive Creation).

Theistic evolution

Probably of the most common origins beliefs is called theistic evolution. As the name implies, it is a blend of theism (belief in God) with standard evolutionary theory. According to this view, God is the initiator but allows everything to unfold and run its course. It incorporates the big bang theory, the chemical origin of life, evolution and common ancestry of all living things, and of course millions of years. It is summarized "God used evolution to create." The only difference between this view and atheistic evolution is that God is involved to some extent.

In large part, theistic evolution is held primarily as a default position. Few churches discuss origins in much depth at all. For Christians who are taught evolution through public schools, universities, museums, media etc, they feel pressure to combine their faith with what they perceive to be the "overwhelming evidence" for evolution. The only logical thing to do is to combine them: perhaps God created through evolution. Such a compromise position can be quite comfortable to individuals who are neither challenged with Scripture nor confronted with many of the problems with evolutionary theory.

Throughout the rest of this book, I will deal with the many challenges to evolutionary theory from scientific arguments and evidence. However, this chapter will be dealing only with Biblical issues and problems related to theistic evolution.

Objections to Theistic Evolution

1. The order of creation does not line up.

At first glance, there may be a superficial overlap between the order of creation in Genesis and that predicted by evolutionary theory. The Biblical text seems to follow an orderly progression with simple creatures being produced first, then more complex ones and then ultimately man. This apparent progression was noted by Francis Collins, Director of the Human Genome Research Institute in a presentation to the ASA where he described how he reconciled science and his faith as theistic evolution:

> "God who is not limited in space or time, who created the universe, chose the remarkable mechanism of evolution to create plants and animals of all sorts. (By the way, notice in Genesis how plants appear before animals and fish before birds—which is precisely what science tells us.)"[6]

However, a closer examination actually reveals a contradictory sequence and the similar progression is ultimately an illusion. Collins has it right that Genesis has plants appearing before animals. However, the evolutionary sequence has numerous marine organisms such as horseshoe crabs millions of years before there are trees which Genesis describes as made on Day 3. (The first animals—fish and birds—are made on Day 5.) While it is correct that both creation and evolution have fish before birds, this

54

agreement is severely weakened by the fact that Genesis has birds being made a full day *before* land animals whereas evolution has land animals first. Importantly, fish are mentioned in Genesis before birds, but both are made on the same day.

Thus, there are significant items that are out of sequential order between the straightforward text of Genesis and the order expected from the theory of evolution. If we were to follow standard theistic evolution, then we must make the assumption that the order of events in Genesis 1 is incorrect. Of the items out of sequence, death is the most relevant and will be discussed later.

Creation	Evolution
Earth first then the sun & moon	Sun first, then earth, then moon
Water first, then land	Land first, then seas
Plants before fish	Fish and marine organisms before plants
Birds before land animals	Reptiles before birds
Death after sin by man	Death ever present

2. Adam and Eve must have been real people.

If we follow evolutionary theory, then the first man would have been born, passed through a birth canal and had a mother, even if she was somehow less than human. Since evolution requires common ancestry and a continuum from the first single celled organism up to man, this does not allow for a real Adam and a real Eve. This is especially true when we consider that the Bible says that man was formed first, and Eve was formed from Adam's rib. The Bible is quite clear that God made Adam "from the dust of the ground" which is why Genesis 3:19 says "…for dust you are and to dust you will return." (NIV) It does not say, "…from apelike ancestors you are and to them you will return."

Several places in Scripture point to Adam and Eve being real people. Adam is included at the end of Jesus' genealogy given in Luke 3:37. When Paul is in Athens, he says "From one man he made every nation of men…" (Acts 17:26 NIV). Paul mentions Eve in 1 Timothy 2:13. Then, in 1 Corinthians 15:22, Paul writes "For as in Adam all die, so in Christ all will be made alive." (NIV) Indeed, there are serious implications to our understanding of salvation and the nature of man if Adam was not a real person.

3. The Fall was a real, historical event.

Importantly, Paul draws this crucial parallel between Adam and Christ: "Consequently, just as the result of one trespass was condemnation for all men, so also the result of one act of righteousness was justification that brings life for all men. For just as through the disobedience of the one man the many were made sinners, so also through the obedience of the one man, the many will be made righteous." Romans 5:18-19 (NIV) Condemnation for all men could only occur through a real Adam after a real Fall. This is necessary for righteousness to also come through one man's obedience.

The significance of this point cannot be understated. It is precisely because of the Fall that we need salvation through Christ Jesus. In God's foreknowledge, he anticipated the Fall and planned for it. When Adam and Eve disobeyed, this was not a surprise to God. Indeed, this is why Revelation 13:8 refers to "the Lamb that was slain from the creation of the world." (NIV) In this way, God shows attributes of his love and mercy that can only be demonstrated through the process of redemption. Because of a very real Fall, the Son of God entered human history, becoming a man just like us. He then took our sins upon himself and suffered death in our place.

4. Death could not occur before the Fall.

Perhaps the most important conflict for theistic evolution is the place of death. The Bible is very clear that death came into the world as a result of man's rebellion and sin. Death is the result of sin and did not precede it. Yet, evolution requires death—millions upon millions of years of it—in order for natural selection to work its magic and have amebas give rise to college students. Indeed evolution by natural selection is not only "survival of the fittest" it is "death of the unfit". This creates serious consequences for our theology.

The very purpose that Jesus Christ came into the world was to defeat death, to take the penalty for sin in our place. The Bible refers to death as "the last enemy to be destroyed." But if death is the means by which God used to create through a process of evolution, then it is not really an enemy. This is exactly where the theory of evolution cuts to the foundation of the Christian faith because it impacts the Gospel. The Gospel only makes sense if Jesus came to pay the death penalty in our place for a real sin.

After the Fall, God made coverings of skin to clothe Adam and Eve in their nakedness. In the process an animal had to die—blood was shed—because "without the shedding of blood there is no forgiveness of sin." (Hebrews 9:22) Likewise, blood was shed to cover the nakedness of our sin. However, this was not the blood of an animal, but the blood of the sinless Lamb of God who takes away the sins of the whole world.

While I was in college, I held to theistic evolution. This seemed to be the only logical conclusion available to a Christian who was studying science. But it was this issue of death before sin that convinced me that theistic evolution could not work. Instead, I began to study the Bible as well as the scientific evidence and saw that Biblical creation was much more tenable.

The quote at the beginning of the chapter from Francis Collins suggests that God could have used evolution to create and asks who are we to say otherwise? While such a response may seem pious and God honoring, in fact, it is neither. God told us in his Word what happened. To insist that creation took place as it says in Genesis does not "put God in a box" as some have suggested. Instead, it takes God at his word.

5. God can't seem to get it right.

Another problem with theistic evolution is that God appears incompetent. Instead of an omnipotent God who calls things into existence, he sits back and watches a random death-driven process. With all of the animals that have gone extinct over billions of years, one would wonder whether God really cared about his creation at all. Nature is red in tooth and claw. Death, disease, bloodshed and survival of the fittest are the nature of evolution. This is totally inconsistent with an omnipotent, loving God that "saw that it was good" after each day of creation. But, we see the opposite in Scripture. God cares about all of his creatures. He is holy, loving, and just and called everything to exist. The reason that there is death and disease in the world is on account of man's sin. **Thus, mutations, death and disease do not indicate an incompetent creator, but an unfortunate necessity in a world that was cursed by God because of man's rebellion.**

In summary, there are significant theological objections that can be raised against the compromise of theistic evolution. Particularly, this view presents conflicts between it and Scripture that are not resolvable. Without a real Adam and Eve, a real Fall, and with sin preceding death, we have lost the very reason that Jesus Christ came into the world. Such a negative impact to the Gospel, (though often unintended by its supporters) has serious consequences.

The Framework Hypothesis

The framework hypothesis is similar to theistic evolution in that it takes a completely non-literal view of Genesis 1-11. It differs from theistic evolution in having a more significant role for God. According to this view, the first chapters of Genesis should not be taken literally at all. Instead, Genesis provides a framework, or literary device that is non-sequential. Thus, even though the text literally says creation took place in six normal days, this is not what really happened. Genesis 1:1-2:3 essentially provides an allegory for us, conveying the important truth that God is the creator. Proponents of this view generally give four major arguments which will be given below and then rebutted.[7]

1. Two triad structure of Genesis 1

If we look at the events of Days 1-3 and compare them to Days 4-6 there are interesting parallels. On Day 1, we have creation of light and darkness. Then, on Day 4 we have the creation of the light bearers. On day 2, we have separation of the water above from the water below the expanse/sky. Then on Day 5 is the creation of the fish and the birds. On Day 3, we have creation of land and plants. Then on Day 6 is the creation of land animals and the man that will take care of the plants. They argue therefore, that Genesis 1 does not provide a sequential account about which came first. Instead, they suggest that Day 4 is not really Day 4, but an elaboration or recapitulation of the first day. It is a topical progression rather than a sequential one.

2. Eternal nature of day 7

The seventh day does not close with an evening and a morning. It is God's rest and it is continuing on into the present. Since this day is not a 24 hour day, then neither are the rest of them. Some who make this argument use Hebrews 4:1-11 for support. This passage is about a Sabbath rest for God's people. This is an ongoing rest and so they assume that God's rest on the seventh day is symbolic and continuing.

3. Anthropomorphisms

There are several anthropomorphisms in the text. God is walking, seeing, speaking, working, resting, and hovering over the waters. Since God does not have physical eyes, feet, a mouth and so on, these are figures of speech and not literally true. Because of such literary devices, this indicates that the whole chapter should not be taken as an actual sequential progression.

4. No rain on earth (Genesis 2:5)

Strangely, another point that they make is to refer to Genesis 2:5 which says that there was no rain on the earth yet. They contend that there must have been rain from the time plants were made if not before. Therefore, since the Bible seems to suggest that there were plants before there was a proper hydrologic cycle, then it must not be providing a sequential timeframe.

Objections to the Framework Hypothesis

1. Parallelism does not rule out a chronological progression.

While it is true that there are some interesting parallels between the first three days and the last three days, this does not rule out a chronological progression. God's purpose in stretching creation out over a period of 7 days is to give us our work week. All of the other time periods are tied to celestial events except the week. This is derived from God's period of creative activity and rest. Since this was God's clear purpose in stretching out creation over a period of six days, we should still expect an ordered progression.

The six day period is not solely derived from Genesis 1. It is also reinforced in Exodus 20:11: "For in six days the LORD made the heavens and the earth, the sea, and all that is in them, but he rested on the seventh day." (NIV) If the creation week was not a real six day period, then why is this point reiterated? This verse reaffirms the fact that creation took place over six normal days.

2. There was a Day 7

The straightforward reading of Genesis 2:2-3 implies that there was a real seventh day, just as the other six days were real. The seventh day is clearly distinct from the others. Just because this portion does not have "evening and morning" does not mean that it must have been a long period of time or that it is continuing. The seventh day is special, it is set apart. The fact that it doesn't follow the same formula "there was evening and morning" does not provide evidence that it did not have an evening and a morning. Absence of evidence is not evidence of absence.

Importantly, there are several indicators that the seventh day was completed. Many of the verbs that are used are past tense. "By the seventh day God had *finished* the work he *had* been doing; so on the seventh day he *rested* from all his work. And God blessed the seventh day and *made* it holy because on it he *rested* from all the work of creating that he *had done*." Genesis 2:2-3 (NIV). Since God "rested" this is an act completed in the past. If it were a present and ongoing task, it should say God "is resting". Moreover, this passage is talking about the seventh day in the past and what happened on that specific day. This is confirmed in Exodus 20:11 "…he rest*ed* on the seventh day." (NIV) If this is an ongoing rather than a completed action, then it should say God "has been resting since the seventh day."

While Hebrews 4:1-11 is talking about entering God's rest, this does not mean that the seventh day is a long period of time. Notice Hebrews 4:10 "for anyone who enters God's rest also rests from his own work, just as God did from his." (NIV) Here again, we see this as a completed rather than an ongoing action. God's resting on the seventh day is different from the Sabbath rest that God's people will enter into which will last forever.

Regardless, there obviously was a seventh day after creation, just as there were Days 1-6. The implication that because there is no evening and morning mentioned for the seventh day means that Days 1-6 spanned potentially millions of years is preposterous.

3. Where does the literary device end?

Singling out the anthropomorphisms applied to God in Genesis 1 and 2 is quite arbitrary. Of course these are literary devices within the text and we should not interpret it to mean that God has physical body parts or needs to rest from all his work. The use of figures of speech and literary devices does not necessarily detract from a historical narrative. If we are going to take such anthropomorphism to imply that a passage of Scripture should not be taken as a sequential, historical account, where would it end? Throughout the entire Bible we see the same notions applied to

God. He speaks, he leads his people with an outstretched arm, he grows angry, and he covers Moses with his hand and then goes past. Again, this does not mean that God must have a physical body. Nonetheless the use of such a literary device does not detract from the historical facts.

4. Plants were watered by mist in the very beginning.[8]

Framework hypothesis proponents need look no further than Genesis 2:6 for the answer to their problem in verse 5: "but streams (mist) came up from the earth and watered the whole surface of the ground" (NIV) Although the Bible indicates that God had not sent rain on the earth at this time, nonetheless, he had provided a means for giving water that the plants needed. Given both of these points, it hardly seems reasonable that the lack of rain before there were plants is any evidence for a non-sequential reading of Genesis 1 and 2. The Bible doesn't tell us how long it was before God did send rain on the earth—only that it was not prior to the creation of man on Day 6.

5. Genesis 1 is historical narrative not poetry

Steven Boyd, a Hebrew scholar from the Master's College has done a fairly comprehensive analysis of the verb tenses in Genesis 1.[9] In Hebrew grammar, **preterite** verbs typify narrative texts. Preterite verbs describe a past action, state or condition. It refers to actions that were *completed* in the past. This verb type tends to be infrequent in poetic passages of Scripture, but dominates in historical narrative. Dr. Boyd's study confirmed the fact that the ratio of preterite verbs in a passage can be used to distinguish the type of passage, whether poetic or historical. Based on this analysis, the verb tenses in Genesis 1 clearly indicate that it is historical and not poetic in nature. This counts as significant evidence against any view that insists that Genesis 1 should be viewed in allegorical, symbolic, poetic or literary frameworks.

Summary of arguments against the framework hypothesis

Although not explicitly stated, a rationale for the framework hypothesis is to accommodate the presumed scientific evidence for long periods of time for the history of the earth and universe. (In later chapters we will address these issues in more depth.) But even here, Framework Hypothesis proponents will run into trouble as they encounter some of the same problems as theistic evolution with the role of death. If Genesis 1 and 2 are allegories and literary devices, is Adam a real person? Was the Fall a real historical event? What about Noah's flood? When does the allegory stop and the true history begin?

As with theistic evolution, the Framework Hypothesis runs into trouble through not approaching Genesis 1-2 as factual history. In particular, issues regarding human origins and the place of death are significant. "...death came through a man..." (1 Corinthians 15:21 NIV) From the Framework Hypothesis, how are we to interpret the fossil record? What are we supposed to do with Neanderthals and *Homo erectus*? (Human origins is dealt with in a later chapter) The Framework Hypothesis addresses the timeframe of Genesis by ignoring the most important consequences of the timeframe. These and other significant theological questions are simply brushed aside with the claim that Genesis 1 is not factual history but a literary device.

In conclusion, while the Framework Hypothesis is an internally consistent model it falls far short on robustness. Indeed, if one is not trying to accommodate millions of years because of presumed scientific evidence, there really is no good rationale for this view. The hermeneutical gymnastics required are completely unjustified without support from alleged scientific evidence that the earth is millions of years old. Further, there is good reason to take Genesis 1 as historical narrative and true history.

The Gap Theory

The Gap Theory is a view that accepts much of Genesis 1-11 as factual history but adds unsupported evidence between the lines. While there are many different versions of the Gap theory, there are a few elements that are common to all of them. For example, all versions insert millions of years between Genesis 1:1 and Genesis 1:2 in order to accommodate the supposed millions of years within the Biblical text. The main premise for this view is that God created a perfect earth in the far distant past where Satan was the ruler of an alleged mineral paradise (Ezekiel 28:12-19). His rebellion (Isaiah 14:12-15) led to judgment and destruction of this world. Some versions of the Gap Theory believe that this destruction was by water to provide the water covering the earth in Genesis 1:2. This is referred to as Lucifer's flood. It is during this judgment and devastation that the fossils and geologic column were supposedly laid down. After this, God *re*created and *re*populated the earth. Thus, the theory is also referred to as the "Ruin—Reconstruction" view. In addition, Gap theorists often suggest that there was a pre-Adamic race—people on earth before Adam and Eve—that were also destroyed in the judgment. Proponents of the Gap theory suggest that the remains of these individuals are the hominid fossils that we find. Some versions of the Gap Theory have the reconstruction roughly 6,000 years ago while the first creation could have been potentially untold millions of years ago.

Thomas Chalmers (1780-1847), a Scottish pastor was one of the early promoters of this view. He claimed that the millions of years could be compatible with the Bible.[10] Later, the Gap Theory was included in footnotes of the *Scofield Reference Bible*. This contributed to the view gaining a much wider following than it otherwise may have. Although more recent editions of *Scofield* have pulled the gap theory footnotes from Genesis, they have found a new home as footnotes in Isaiah.

Like the Framework Hypothesis, one of the main reasons for the Gap Theory is to accommodate the millions of years that so many scientists have insisted are necessary. Indeed, Gap theorists can say, "take all the time that you want, we'll just put it here between verse 1 and 2 of Genesis 1. Whether they acknowledge it or not, the major reason for adopting this position is the alleged evidence of millions of years as it does not come from a straightforward reading of the Genesis text.

Since the gap in the time is supposed to occur between verses 1 and 2, much of the evidence is pulled from Genesis 1:2. This verse in the NIV reads, "Now the earth was formless and empty, darkness was upon the face of the deep." (NIV) Gap theorists prefer the translation "And then the earth became without form and void, darkness was upon the face of the deep." Notice how this later interpretation of the Hebrew text fits the Gap Theory better. Let's take a look at whether this interpretation is warranted and other arguments that are used to support the Gap theory and their objections.[11]

Gap Theory arguments

1. Without form and void

The Hebrew words *tohu* and *bohu* can be translated as without form and void. Gap theorists insist that this implies destruction and judgment. For support, they appeal to two other passages where these two words are found together: Jeremiah 4:23 and Isaiah 34:11.

> "I looked at the earth, and it was *formless* and *empty*; and at the heavens and their light was gone." Jeremiah 4:23 (NIV)

> "…God will stretch out over Edom the measuring line of *chaos* and the plumb line of *desolation.*" Isaiah 34:11 (NIV)

In both of these cases, the terms are used in the context of judgment. Therefore, Gap theorists interpret Genesis 1:2 as implying God's judgment here as well. Further, since *tohu* can mean chaos, they ask; how could God create something that was chaotic? They argue that it must have been initially perfect and

65

then destroyed. In the destruction, it could be chaotic and then restored or refurbished.

As further evidence regarding this, they also point to Isaiah 45:18:

> "For this is what the LORD says—he who created the heavens, he is God; he who fashioned and made the earth, he founded it; he did not create it to be *empty*, but formed it to be inhabited..." (NIV)

The argument here is that the earth was not created to be *empty* (tohu). Since the earth was "empty" in Genesis 1:2, it must have *become* that way temporarily following God's judgment.

2. The Earth <u>became</u> without form and void

Gap theorists prefer to translate the Hebrew verb *hayetha* as "became" instead of "was" in Genesis 1:2 because that better fits with their interpretive framework. There is no textual evidence or arguments that support this position. The reason for this interpretation is to imply a temporal sequence.

3. "And then" vs. "Now"

In the same way, gap theorists prefer to use what is called a *waw* consecutive as the link between verses 1 and 2. This occurs in normal story telling and denotes a sequential activity. Such a word would be translated as "and", "then" or "and then". It is conveying an ordered sequence of events. Since gap proponents believe that the earth was created, judged, destroyed, and then reformed. It makes perfect sense to them that this should be translated "and then" instead of "Now" or simply "and".

4. Created (*bara*) vs. Made (*asah*)

In Hebrew, there are two terms **bara** and **asah** that have to do with creation. *Bara* is used essentially of God's activity alone and implies a creation that includes the very material. When God creates, he calls the material into existence. This is contrasted with

66

asah which suggests making from something else. This is the same sense as a sculptor who makes a statue from stone. He *makes* the statute out of the stone; he doesn't *create* the stone with the statute. Since *bara* is used infrequently in Genesis 1, it must be that this is a recreation or formation using some preexisting materials.

Exodus 20:11 is a serious challenge to Gap Theory proponents. "For in six days the LORD made the heavens and the earth, the sea and all that is in them...." (NIV) This comprehensive verse clearly states that the creation of the heavens, the earth, and the sea all occurred in six days. While we might expect this to settle the matter, gap theorists get around this. Since the verb used is *asah* (made), they interpret this to mean that the *re*-creation took place in a six day period. In other words, it took God six days to make the earth and everything in it *after* he had already created it in the distant past and then judged it. Even though this may seem like a significant stretch, I have actually had conversations with people who argued this very point.

Objections and Rebuttals to the Gap Theory

1. The use of *tohu* and *bohu* does not imply God's judgment.

The words tohu and bohu are not always used in the context of judgment. The meanings "formless and empty", "unformed and unfilled", "without form and void" do not mean chaotic nor do they mean destroyed. A straightforward interpretation of the phrase is that God created an earth that was initially unformed and unfilled, but was soon to be both *formed* and *filled*. Since it was exactly the way God wanted it at the end of the first day, it is still "very good" even if it is not yet filled.

The passages mentioned in Jeremiah 4:23 and Isaiah 34:11 describe a future destruction and judgment of God. It seems more appropriate to use the context the first time a word is used and apply it to later times rather than the other way around. Therefore, we might better interpret the destruction prophesied in Jeremiah and Isaiah to be devastation so bad as to make it in the same condition as the earth before it was habitable. In other words, the destruction would be like the earth before there was anything on it. Gap theorists do the opposite and apply a prophesied devastation as the context for the first occurrence of the phrase even though there is nothing else in Genesis 1:2 that would imply judgment.

The word *tohu* is translated in the following ways in the NIV: "nothing," "empty," "formless," "waste," "barren," "chaos," "confusion," "empty space," "false," "in vain," "ruined," "useless," "useless idols," "wasteland" and "worthless." Apart from it being used to describe what God will destroy in Isaiah and Jeremiah, there is nothing to suggest that the term conveys an implied judgment in Genesis 1:2.

In the same way, *bohu* is translated as "empty" and "desolation" in the very few times that it is found in the Old Testament. Again, there is nothing that adds judgment apart from it being used twice in a prophesied description of devastation. Use of a term in a context sheds light on its meaning in other contexts. However, it doesn't necessarily carry the *context* to every other occurrence. Just because it is used in the context of judgment does not mean that it carries judgment with it every time it is used.

2. "Was" not "Became"

There is nothing in the text to suggest that the Hebrew verb *hayetha* in Genesis 1:2 should be translated as "became." Virtually every occurrence of the word alone it is translated as "was." In contrast, the normal way to express "became" is to add the preposition "to" to the verb "was". This combination is properly translated as became.

3. "Now" means "Now"

In Hebrew, when "and" (*waw*) is joined to a verb, it is called a *waw* **consecutive**. It conveys sequential information and is the normal story telling form. In contrast, if it is joined to a noun, it adds additional information as a noun clause, a *waw* **disjunctive**. In Genesis 1:2, *waw* is connected to "the earth" and is therefore part of a noun clause. A noun clause is simultaneous and adds further information about the state of the noun. It does not convey

68

a sequential ordering. The NIV translation imputes the contemporary nature by the use of "now" instead of "and" in Genesis 1:2.

The other verses that are translated "now" include:

"*Now* the LORD God had planted a garden..."Genesis 2:8 (NIV)

"*Now* the LORD God had formed out of the ground..."Genesis 2:19 (NIV)

Notice that in both of these verses what is being added is additional information not sequential information. In most of the other verses in Genesis 1, *waw* is attached to the verb and is conveying sequential information. Another example of this in English is the phrase "by the way." This informs the reader that there is *additional* information and it is a departure from the main point.

4. "Created" and "Made" are used interchangeably.

Unlike the gap theorists' assumption, there is no clear distinction between the meaning of "created" and the meaning of "made." In fact, the words are used interchangeably just as they are in English. Throughout the Bible, it says "God created X" and "God made X" where X is the same for both.

	Created (*bara*)	Made (*asah*)
Heavens and Earth	Gen 1:1	Exodus 20:11
	Gen 2:4	Psalm 115:15
		Isaiah 37:16
Heavens only	Isaiah 45:18	
	Isaiah 42:5	
Earth only		Isaiah 45:18
Stars	Psalm 148:5	Gen 1:16
Sea creatures	Gen 1:21	Exodus 20:11
Man	Gen 1:27	Gen 1:26
	Gen 5:1, 2	Gen 5:1
	Gen 6:7	Gen 6:6

The interchangeability becomes especially apparent in Genesis 5:1 where it says "When God *created* (*bara*) man, he *made* (*asah*) him in the likeness of God." (NIV) And again in Genesis 6:6-7 "The LORD was grieved that he had *made* (*asah*) man…So the LORD said, 'I will wipe mankind, whom I have *created* (*bara*)…'" (NIV)

Therefore, since both *bara* and *asah* are used for the same objects and even used alternately in sequential verses and even the same verse, there is not a clear distinction between them. This would suggest that the gap theorists' insistence that they are distinct and imply a recreation is severely misplaced.

5. The new heavens and the new earth.

If there was a previous world that was destroyed then we would be living on the second earth. This runs into trouble when we look at Revelation 21:1. "Then I saw a new heaven and a new earth, for the first heaven and the first earth had passed away…" (NIV) If this is the second earth as the gap theorists' claim, then it should say that the "second earth" passed away not the first.

6. God leaves a righteous remnant after judgment

The pattern throughout the Scripture is to have a righteous remnant every time God passes judgment. This occurred whether it was the Flood, Sodom and Gomorrah, Jericho, etc. If the pre-Adamic race was judged and that world destroyed it is the only time *without* a righteous remnant. This is inconsistent with the Biblical patter of a righteous remnant that is spared from God's judgment.

7. The original creation was "very good"

In Genesis 1:31, God describes his creation as "very good." This hardly would be the case with the fall of Satan and a ruined/reconstructed heavens and earth. The Gap Theory also has judgment and death before the Fall of Adam and Eve. The Bible is very clear that it is Adam's sin that brought sin and death into the world and thus God's judgment.

70

After careful consideration of the way the Hebrew should be translated from Genesis 1, it becomes apparent that the translation supporting the Gap Theory was done to accommodate a gap of millions of years instead of naturally flowing from the text.

Progressive Creation and Day/Age Theory

The remaining two creation compromise positions will be dealt with together. Because there is a wide range of views and some overlap between Progressive Creation and the Day/Age theory they will be discussed together. Additionally, the same objections apply to both of these theories. Depending on the individual who holds these positions, they may take more or less of Genesis literally. What these views all have in common is rejecting the "days" of Genesis 1 as normal 24 hour days.

Progressive Creation, also called Process Creation, may be more or less similar to theistic evolution depending on how much the individual believes that God was involved in the process. For example, some proponents believe in the big bang theory and millions of years. At the same time, they may also believe that Adam and Eve were real people, the Fall was a historical event and Noah's Flood was a real, global catastrophe. In contrast, others may believe or reject different combinations of these and other tenets. They typically hold that God created major life forms in progressive stages with long periods of time in which they diversified by evolutionary mechanisms. Unfortunately, even many prominent Christian leaders hold to this compromise view. As will be discussed later, this creates an immediate conflict with Scripture. The Bible says that God made the sun, moon and stars on Day 4. Thus, it contradicts the big bang theory which would have stars made billions of years before the earth.

Some progressive creationists believe in varying degrees of common ancestry. (Common ancestry is a major component of evolutionary theory and will be covered in chapter 5.) For example, they may accept the fact that reptiles gave rise to birds as suggested by the theory of evolution. In other words, God created birds through the process of evolution from reptiles. Thus, progressive creationists have more room for God in the creative

71

process than theistic evolutionists. Many of the arguments against theistic evolution would apply to progressive creation as well.

Day/Age theory proponents tend to be more conservative than Progressive Creationists and take more of Genesis 1-11 as literal history. However, they view the days of Genesis 1 as corresponding to long periods of time—even up to millions of years or the geologic ages. One of the more common versions of the Day/Age theory suggests that each of the days mentioned in Genesis 1 are 1,000 years long. Those who hold to this view tend to take much more of Genesis literally than those that would be progressive creationists. Again, in this area there is often a continuum and variety of beliefs

To counter these views, many of the arguments addressed previously in this chapter apply. However, in this case it is necessary to specifically focus on the length of the days in Genesis 1. Issues related to the age of the earth will be considered in chapter 6. Here, the focus is on the length of the days.

Arguments to support the "days" of Genesis 1 as normal days

1. A day is not a thousand years

One of the most common versions of the Day/Age theory contends that the days of Genesis 1 are long periods of time, most likely 1,000 years in length. There are significant problems with this idea. The notion comes from 2 Peter 3:8 "With the Lord a day is like a thousand years…" (NIV) and is reinforced by Psalm 90:4 "For a thousand years in your sight are like a day that has just gone by, or like a watch in the night." (NIV) So, they take this information and apply it to Genesis 1 to conclude that each day is 1,000 years.

Such a view is problematic for a number of reasons. First of all, both of these verses are really using a figure of speech. A simile is a comparison that uses 'like' or 'as.' This is clear in each verse. It does not say, "a day is *equal* to 1,000 years" but that it is '*like* a 1,000 years. If we check the full context of these verses we would see this reinforced. The purpose in both passages is to demonstrate

72

and describe God's patience. God does not measure time the way that man does. A long time to us goes very quickly to God. Second, the rest of the verse in 2 Peter cancels it out: "...and a thousand years are like a day." (NIV) If a day is like a thousand years and a thousand years are like a day, then you can't say that the days in Genesis are 1,000 years long.

An additional flaw in the argument is the fact that plants are made on Day 3 (before the sun on Day 4 and the insects that pollinate them on Day 5/6). This creates a problem. If each of the days were 1,000 years long, this would make an evening and a morning (the night/day cycle) 500 years apiece. This will not be good for the plants to be in darkness for so long. The only solution around this problem is to suggest that there were many day/night cycles. However, this runs up against the "there was evening and there was morning." What is the evening and morning of a thousand years or a million years?

2. Use of the Hebrew word for day (*yom*)

Much of the controversy regarding the length of the days of Genesis 1 centers on the meaning of the Hebrew word *yom*. Day/Age advocates have made much of the fact that this word can have several different meanings including long periods of time. Indeed *yom* can have the following meanings among others:

- The light period during the day/night cycle as in "the greater light to govern the *day*."(Genesis 1:16)
- A period of 24 hours or a specific day as in "the twenty-seventh *day* of the second month" (Genesis 8:14)
- A lifetime as in "his *days* will be a hundred and twenty years" (Genesis 6:3)
- When or "in the day of" as in "This is the account of the heavens and the earth *when* they were created." (Genesis 2:4)

Thus, while *yom* can have several different meanings, it is not difficult to tell from the context which meaning is appropriate. Of course we would never be confused by how many *days* Jonah was

73

in the belly of the fish, or how many *days* the Israelites marched around Jericho. The only place people seem to be confused about the meaning of the word *yom* is in Genesis 1 and this is only because of the supposed evidence of millions of years for the age of the earth.

All of the evidence from lexicons and dictionaries demonstrate that the proper interpretation of the six days in Genesis 1 is normal, solar days. This was emphasized by James Barr, a prominent Hebrew scholar. Although Barr did not believe in Biblical inerrancy, nonetheless, he thought it was abundantly clear what the intent of the author of Genesis 1 was. He wrote:

> "...probably, so far as I know, there is no professor of Hebrew or Old Testament at any world-class university who does not believe that the writer(s) of Genesis 1-11 intended to convey to their readers the ideas that:
> (a) creation took place in a series of six days which were the same days of 24 hours that we now experience,
> (b) the figures contained in the Genesis genealogies provided by simple addition a chronology from the beginning of the world up to later stages in the biblical story,
> (c) Noah's flood was understood to be worldwide and extinguish all human and animal life except for those in the ark."[12]

Importantly, Barr did not *believe* that this was what happened; only that it was the clear meaning and intent of the author. This makes him a more reliable source for the interpretation. He is not trying to force an interpretation on the text since his personal bias and belief is the opposite.

3. Non-literal vs. literal meanings of Yom

When *yom* is meant to imply a period longer than a day, it is always found with prepositions, prepositional phrases and other types of formulas and constructs or it is used in the plural.

74

However, when *yom* is meant to convey a normal day, it is singular, always joined to a numeral, and used as a plain noun (not with prepositions, prepositional phrases etc.)

In Genesis 1, *yom* is used in the singular, with a number, and without prepositions for each of the six days. Thus, there is strong contextual evidence that each of these days should be viewed as normal, singular days. When *yom* is used for "daylight" and "when", the context is clearly different. In addition, these days are double labeled with the phrase "there was evening and there was morning..." The phrase by itself carries with it the meaning of one day.

There are two verses that have been held up as exceptions where *yom* is used with a number and yet alleged to mean something other than a normal day. These are Zechariah 14:7 and Hosea 6:2.

> "It will be a *unique day*, without daytime or nighttime—a day known to the LORD. When evening comes, there will be light" Zechariah 14:7 (NIV)

> "After two *days* he will revive us; on the third *day* he will restore us, that we may live in his presence." Hosea 6:2.

Notice how both of these passages have a prophetic rather than a historical context. The unique day of Zechariah is clearly meant to be a special day. In a sense, it appears to refer to the "day of the LORD" and certainly is not referring to the six days of creation at all. Thus, there is nothing in this usage that would contradict the interpretation of the six days of creation as meaning normal days.

In addition to being prophetic, the verse in Hosea follows a common Hebrew idiom. It has the formula N; N+1, where N represents a number of items and N+1 represents a number increased by one. This is an expression that is found especially in Proverbs and Ecclesiastes. ("There are six things the LORD hates, seven that are detestable to him..." Proverbs 6:16 (NIV)) Although this seems to be a case where *yom* is used with a number and yet means a longer period of time, it is not necessarily so. If it is interpreted as specifically referring to two days and a third day,

75

this would not harm the text or alter the apparent meaning. The passage is a call to repentance which should never take a long period of time. Further, it has been suggested that this passage can be interpreted as a prophecy regarding the resurrection of Christ. If that is true, then it would mean that even in this case, the correct rendering is three normal days. Still, there is nothing here that harkens back to the creation week. Even if these two verses are exceptions to *yom*+numeral = normal day it does not detract from the overwhelming evidence that the proper rendering of *yom* in the six days of Genesis 1 is normal days.

Importantly, while there are many different time-related words or word combinations that could have been used to indicate long periods of time, only one word has a meaning of a normal day: *yom*. Isn't it interesting that this is the word that is chosen? This hardly seems coincidental.

When we consider the evidence that suggests that the intent of the author was to convey six normal 24 hour periods, we should also look again at Exodus 20:11: "For in six days the LORD made the heavens and the earth, the sea, and all that is in them, but he rested on the seven day. Therefore the LORD blessed the Sabbath day and made it holy." (NIV) Deuteronomy 9:10 indicates that the Ten Commandments were written in stone "by the finger of God." Therefore, it is God himself that wrote: *"in six days"*. This fact should cause us to pause if we try to interpret it as *more* than six days.

Challenges to the Normal Day Interpretation of Genesis 1

1. How long were days before the sun was made?

Apart from appeals to the scientific evidence for millions of years, the biggest challenge to the normal day interpretation of Genesis 1 is probably the length of the days before the sun was made on Day 4. This is troubling for some because they don't understand how there can be 24 hr days without the sun. However, even here, the normal day interpretation has a solid exegesis. First of all, if we accept the premise that the sun was made on Day 4,

76

then we have *de facto* rejected the big bang theory and all of the astronomical evidence for billions of years. According to the big bang theory stars were made well before the earth. These stars then exploded and produced the heavy elements necessary to form the earth. This is quite incompatible with the Bible which has plants on earth on Day 3 before the sun, moon and stars were made.

There are several reasons that this is not a significant challenge to the normal day interpretation. First, God created light and separated it from darkness on the first day. This means that there could be a period of light and a period of darkness from the beginning even without the sun. Second, God controls the light and the darkness. During the plagues of Egypt, one of the plagues was that of darkness. Wherever the Egyptians were, they were in total darkness, yet in the same country the Israelites had light where they were. In addition, in Revelation 21:23 it says: "The city does not need the sun or the moon to shine on it, for the glory of God gives it light, and the Lamb is its lamp." (NIV) Thus, God himself could provide light during the first three days without the sun and moon.

A criticism against the sun being formed after the earth is the effect of gravity and the earth's rotation. Obviously, the scientific evidence we have about gravity shows that there would be dramatic effects on the earth if the sun appeared or disappeared. If the earth stopped in its rotation, we would likewise have problems. A counter to this may be Joshua's long day. In Joshua 10:12-14, the sun stood still in the sky in the middle of the day and delayed going down about a full day. We also have the reversal of the shadow during the reign of Hezekiah. While it is unclear exactly what happened in these cases and they could have been local rather than global miracles, it reinforces the same fact. **The God who created the sun and appointed it to "govern the day" is not bothered by gravity or the motion of the sun and planets.** When he commands, they stop, and everything on earth doesn't fly off the planet. From these and the other miracles of God, we know that he is not bound by the physical laws which he has established.

Because of the importance we attach to the sun, it does seem surprising that it was not made first. However, if we consider the fact that many ancient people worshiped the sun, moon and stars, this may give us some insight into God's purpose in delay. What better way to show that these celestial bodies are not very significant than to create them well after creation on earth is underway. In addition, the sun and moon are neither named nor blessed by God whereas essentially everything else made during that week was named or blessed. They are simply called "two great lights" which does seem like an understatement. Another understatement refers to the stars. There are billions and billions of stars in the universe and they can be the size of hundreds of earths. When the Bible speaks of God creating them, it is almost like, "Oh, yeah. He made the stars also." It is a passing comment. As big and as numerous as these stars are, they simply give us a perspective of how much bigger and greater is our God who called them to existence.

2. Where did Cain get his wife?

Another common criticism that is often mockingly leveled against Biblical creation is: Where did Cain get his wife? In fact, this question was one of the ones that William Jennings Bryan was asked while on the witness stand during the Scopes Trial in 1925. Unfortunately, Bryan could not give an answer.[13] While this question has stumped a good many people, it does not need to. The Bible is very clear that all people are descendants of Adam and have inherited their sinful nature from him. In addition, Adam "named his wife Eve because she would become the mother of all the living." (Genesis 3:20 NIV) Since Adam "had other sons and daughters" (Genesis 5:4) the obvious conclusion is that Cain's wife was one of his sisters. The only other possibility would be a niece, but this is less likely.

At first consideration the idea that Cain's wife was a sister sounds crazy. (Especially if we think about our brothers and sisters!) However, there really would not have been much choice. At that time in history and also shortly after the Flood, there would not have been any option besides marrying such close relatives. This does seem very strange to us, but we should look at some other passages in Genesis. Abraham's wife, Sarah, was also his half sister. They had the same father, but different mothers (Genesis 20:12) In addition, Nahor (Abraham's brother) took his niece Milcah to be his wife. Abraham's son Isaac married Rebekah who was the granddaughter of Nahor and Milcah. Isaac's son Jacob married Rachel and Leah who were the daughters of Laban. Laban was his uncle (his mother's brother) and thus they were his first cousins. Apparently, there were different considerations in the early stages of human history. We must remember that this was at a time before significant numbers of mutations had accumulated in the human gene pool. Thus, there would not have been the same deleterious effects of concentrating recessive mutations as can occur today.

There are significant consequences to the Gospel if we accept a premise other than Cain's wife was his sister. If we assume that God made other people or there were other people around at the time, then this impacts our understanding of the Fall and salvation. People who were not a descendant of Adam would not have inherited a sin nature from him. They would not have had a blood relationship to Christ Jesus who is also a descendant of Adam.

An issue related to the question of Cain's wife is: Who was Cain afraid of after he killed Abel? Cain was worried that someone would kill him and expressed this concern to God. Then God put a mark on Cain so that no one would kill him. Because Cain was afraid, it implies that there were a lot of people around that could have killed him. This poses a problem if one assumes that the only people on earth at the time were Adam, Eve, Cain and Abel. However, this does not take into account when Abel's murder took place. Adam was 130 years old when Seth was born and Eve viewed him as a replacement for Abel (Genesis 4:25). Therefore, it is likely that the death of Abel was close to 130 years after creation. Adam and Eve easily could have had dozens of children and perhaps many grandchildren by this time. It is possible that there was a sizable number of people at the time that Cain killed his brother. All of them would have been descendants of Adam and Eve.

3. What about the dinosaurs?

People also wonder what to do with the dinosaurs if creation took place in six normal days. If we accept the Genesis timeframe, then this would mean that dinosaurs and people lived at the same time. **All land animals were made on the sixth day which is the same day as man**. Thus, although many animals have gone extinct over the years, their ancestors coexisted with man in the past.

Some of the evidence that man and dinosaurs may have lived at the same time are the dragon legends that are held all over the world by different cultures. These may represent the faded descriptions of the interaction of men and dinosaurs. The fact that they were called dragons instead of dinosaurs is not a problem. We must remember that the term 'dinosaur' was not used until 1842. Therefore, we would not expect them to be called dinosaurs historically. Nonetheless, the descriptions are similar.

In the book of Job, there are descriptions of two animals that are probably what we would consider dinosaurs: the behemoth and the leviathan.

> "Look at *behemoth*, which I made along with you and which feeds on grass like an ox. What strength he has in his loins, what power in the muscles of his belly! His tail sways like a cedar; the sinews of his thighs are close knit."
> Job 40:15-17 (NIV)

Interestingly, the footnote for behemoth in the NIV suggests "Possibly a hippopotamus or the elephant" However, this hardly seems reasonable since the tail of both of these animals could never be confused with that of a cedar. On the other hand a cedar is an excellent description of a dinosaur tail.

Conclusion

There are a wide range of views of Genesis that compromise with various aspects of evolutionary theory and millions of years. In so doing, each one encounters some serious challenges from the plain reading of the Genesis text. Another significant problem is having death in the world before sin. Further, it is necessary that Adam and Eve were real people and the Fall was a real historic event. Strong evidence supports the normal day interpretation of the six days of creation. Therefore, millions of years cannot be placed during the creation week or before it as in the Gap Theory. Biblical (young earth) creation provides a robust account of creation and makes the most sense of the data. Apart from the supposed scientific evidence for an old earth there is essentially nothing that argues for an old age for the earth and universe. Instead, the Bible makes a compelling case for creation during a period of six normal days.

Often, the claim is made that evolution does not conflict with faith in God or with the Bible. This claim is usually made by Christians in science such as Francis Collins or theologians with a passion for science. To insist that God could use evolution or that the Bible is compatible with evolution, they must ignore the role of death, all of the objections to long periods of time raised here, and the text of Genesis itself. Those who interpret Genesis as an allegory do serious damage and once that door is opened, there is no clear place to stop. From a Biblical perspective, evolution and millions of years cannot be reconciled with Genesis.

---

[1] Francis Collins quoted in "God is 'the greatest scientist there is'" Dallas Morning News July 26, 2006
http://www.fortwayne.com/mld/newssentinel/15125578.htm

[2] Martin Luther in Jaroslav Peliken, editor, "Luther's Works," *Lectures on Genesis Chapters 1-5*, Vol. 1 (St. Louis: Concordia Publishing House, 1958), pp. 3.

[3] Ibid pp 5

[4] Ibid, pp 5.

[5] Ussher, James 1658. *The Annals of the World*, Revised and Updated by Larry and Marion Pierce, Master Books 2003.

[6] Collins, Francis S. 2003. Faith and the Human Genome *Perspectives on Science and Christian Faith* **55**(3):142-153.

[7] For arguments in support of the framework hypothesis see: The Report of the Committee to Study the Framework Hypothesis Presented to the Presbytery of Southern California (OPC) at its Meeting on October 15-16, 1999 online at
http://www.asa3.org/gray/framework/frameworkOPC-SC.html
A rebuttal of the Framework Hypothesis is: Pipa, J.A. From Chaos to Cosmos: A Critique of the Framework Hypothesis http://capo.org/cpc/pipa.htm

[8] This should not be taken to mean that there was no rain until the flood. The Bible does not say that. It only says that the Lord had not yet sent rain at the time of these events which were apparently all on Day 6.

[9] Steven Boyd's research is presented in DeYoung, D. Thousands… Not Billions published by Master Books 2005 Chapter 10.

[10] Sarfati, Jonathan, 2004. Refuting Compromise Master Books 2004 p.135

[11] I would like to thank Dr. Harvey Hartman for notes regarding the Gap Theory. An excellent rebuttal to the gap theory is the book "Unformed and Unfilled" by W. W. Fields.

[12] J. Barr, letter to David C.C. Watson, April 23, 1984 as quoted in Sarfati, Jonathan, 2004. Refuting Compromise Master Books p.135

[13] Transcript of the Scopes Trial, Monday July 20, 1925.

4

Billions of Dead Things

"I have set my rainbow in the clouds, and it will be the sign of the covenant between me and the earth. Whenever I bring clouds over the earth and the rainbow appears in the clouds, I will remember my covenant between me and you and all living creatures of every kind. Never again will the waters become a flood to destroy all life. Whenever the rainbow appears in the clouds, I will see it and remember the everlasting covenant between God and all living creatures of every kind on the earth." Genesis 9:13-16 (NIV)

According to the Bible, God destroyed the world with a flood which killed all of the people and animals except those which were with Noah on the ark. The Flood of Noah, with the tremendous population bottleneck and subsequent repopulation of the earth, has had a tremendous impact on biology. Most of the species and genetic diversity of the Pre-Flood world was lost and the genetic information remaining was limited and concentrated into just a few individuals of each kind of animal. During and after the Flood, we would expect significant geological changes to the earth including plate tectonics, and changes in weather that may have climaxed in the Ice Age. Such a catastrophe would have left a mark in history as a warning for future generations. Thus, a world-wide global flood would have certainly left *geological*, *biological* and *historical* evidence.

The reason that God sent the Flood is spelled out in Genesis 6:

"The LORD saw how great man's wickedness on the earth had become and that every inclination of the thoughts of his heart

83

was only evil all the time. The LORD was grieved that he had made man and his heart was filled with pain. So the LORD said, 'I will wipe mankind, whom I have created, from the face of the earth—men and animals, and creatures that move along the ground, and birds of the air—for I am grieved that I have made them.'" Genesis 6:5-7 NIV.

"Now the earth was corrupt in God's sight and was full of violence. God saw how corrupt the earth had become, for all the people on earth had corrupted their ways. So God said to Noah, 'I am going to put an end to all people, for the earth is filled with violence because of them. I am surely going to destroy both them and the earth." Genesis 6:11-13 NIV.

Thus, the Flood was the result of God's judgment against evil and the sinfulness of mankind. It stands as a testimony both of God's wrath poured out because of sin and of God's mercy in saving a righteous remnant in Noah and his family.

Since Noah's Flood plays a major role in our understanding of the world from a creationist perspective, it comes as no surprise that the account of the Flood in Genesis has come under attack.

Those who criticize Noah's Flood often take one of three different approaches. First, some completely deny that anything like the Flood ever took place and it is completely mythological. Second, others insist that while some kind of localized flood did occur in the ancient world it did not cover the entire earth. Those who believe in a localized flood may do so from a secular perspective and assume evidence for a flood near the Mediterranean Sea formed the basis of the "legend" of Noah's Flood. The third approach appears more Biblical; however, it still assumes that Noah's Flood was only a local event. An example of someone who advocates the later is Hugh Ross of *Reasons to Believe*.

"Reasons to Believe scholars make a solid case from the Bible that Noah's Flood was "universal," impacting the entire human race and all animals associated with humanity, without necessarily being global. Given RTBs belief that early humans failed to spread out over the planet the flood need not have extended beyond the Mesopotamian area. RTB clearly affirms belief that Noah's Flood wiped out all of humanity in existence at the time, with the lone exception of Noah and his family."[1]

It is important to note that the term "universal" used above and in quotation marks in the original uses a special definition of the term. In other words, from the perspective of the people in the Middle East where all of the people were, the "whole world" was destroyed by the Flood. However, the whole world (from North Pole to South Pole) was not really affected. Therefore, Noah's Flood was not truly universal in extent. As will be shown below, such a strained view of Genesis does not really fit with the scientific or the Biblical evidence. Moreover, a key assumption of this view is that "early humans failed to spread out over the planet." This assumption has no basis in Scripture and in fact the opposite might be implied as God said, "I am going to put an end to all people, for the earth is *filled* with violence because of them." (Genesis 6:13) It would appear that the rationale Reasons to Believe uses for their assumption is to allow for the pre-determined conclusion: a local flood.

Generally speaking, those who hold to an old earth perspective tend to be dismissive of Noah's Flood or assume that it was only a localized phenomenon. Old earth views are difficult to reconcile with Noah's Flood as a truly global event. This is because the geologic column is either evidence of millions of years *or* evidence of a globe covering flood. It cannot be both. **Since the geologic column with its million year time frames is used as evidence that the earth is old, it cannot also be used as geological evidence for Noah's Flood.** Likewise, if the strata and geologic column was laid down quickly during and shortly after the globe-covering flood, then the geologic evidence of the millions of years evaporates. Because a truly globe covering flood *would* leave geologic evidence, the old earth creationist is bound to reject a global flood. The alternative, (if the geologic column demonstrates millions of years) is to have a globe-covering flood that left no geologic evidence. This would truly be a miracle.

Secular criticisms of the Flood often focus on two areas: the water and the ark itself. People often question where all of the water came from in order to cover the earth and then also question where all of the water went. The Bible tells us plainly where the water came from. Of course some of the water came from "...the flood gates of the heavens were opened. And rain fell on the earth for forty days and forty nights." Genesis 7:11-12. There was also water that came when "the springs of the great deep burst forth."

While we don't know exactly what these springs were, they no doubt would have provided significant amounts of water. Possible sources include geysers, volcanoes, or deep sea vents. Each of these would provide hot water that could come out from under the surface of the earth. Further, there is still a significant amount of ground water that is under the earth's surface—perhaps more than in all of the lakes and rivers above the earth. Therefore significant amounts of water could have come from under the surface of the earth. Heating of this water could have contributed to significant evaporation and subsequent rainfall.

As far as where the water went, *it is still here*! Roughly 70% of the earth's surface is covered with water. The ocean basins are extremely deep—so deep in fact that there are underwater mountain ranges that would dwarf even the highest mountain ranges that are on land. The mountains on the continents probably rose greatly during and after the Flood as mountain ranges in the pre-Flood world may not have been as high as today.

Noah's ark was not a typical shape and size for a boat. The dimensions given in Scripture describe a somewhat rectangular vessel. Importantly, the size of which (450 feet long, 75 feet wide, and 45 feet high) would provide the equivalent volume of roughly 520 railroad box cars. This is huge by any stretch of the imagination. It certainly was more than adequate to carry representative pairs of organisms to repopulate the earth.[2] John Woodmorappe has written a study on the feasibility of the ark based on size and estimates of the number of animals involved.[3]

Evidence that Noah's Flood was global

1. Testimony of the Bible itself

Even if the ark was ever found, this would only be the second best evidence for believing the Flood happened. The best evidence

86

is the Scripture itself. Jesus Christ himself acknowledged the Flood mentioning Noah and the Flood: "Just as it was in the days of Noah....Then the flood came and destroyed them all" Luke 17:26-27. This is further confirmed by Peter who mentions the Flood also:

"'Ever since our fathers died everything goes on as it has since the beginning of creation.' But they deliberately forget....By these waters also the world of that time was deluged and destroyed." II Peter 3:4b-6

Thus, the writers of the Bible indicate no doubt or question that the events described in Genesis 6-9 were real events in history

2. The divine purpose of the Flood

The purpose of the Flood was to "wipe mankind, whom I have created, from the face of the earth—men and animals." Thus, the purpose was to start over. If the whole earth was not going to be covered, it would make more sense to *move* instead of build such a huge boat. Indeed, why have all of the animals on board the ark for a year if only those from a localized area would be in jeopardy. Further, since the ark was afloat for an entire year, why would it take so long to reach dry land if the Flood was localized to the region of Mesopotamia? Moreover, the first dove sent out to see if the water had receded came back because it "could find no place to rest its feet."

With potentially millions of people at the time of Noah, it seems unrealistic to believe that they had not spread out over much of the whole earth. God's command had been to "fill the earth and subdue it." This point is echoed in Genesis 6:11-13 with "the earth was *full* of violence" and the "earth is filled with violence." The implication is that man had spread over the earth and brought violence with him. The objective of the Flood is spelled out in Genesis 6:17: "I am going to bring flood waters on the earth to destroy all life under the heavens, every creature that has the breath of life in it. Everything on earth will perish." The reiteration and use of 'every' and 'all' are inconsistent with a localized, limited disaster.

87

3. God's covenant to never again destroy all life with a flood.

The beautiful rainbows that we see are God's reminders that He would not destroy the world again with water. However, there have been numerous local floods that have been devastating. In particular, the tsunami that hit Southeast Asia in December, 2004 is a prime example. Thousands of people died in this tragedy. Hurricane Katrina in 2005 and other hurricanes have caused considerable damage and loss of life through flooding. Although there have been many local floods in earth history, there has only been one truly global flood.

4. All the animals died in the Flood

The description of the events of the Flood does not leave open the possibility that there were animals elsewhere on the globe that were protected. Actually, any other interpretation is a serious distortion of the Biblical text.

> "*Every* living thing that moved on the earth perished—birds, livestock, wild animals, *all* the creatures that swarm over the earth, and all mankind. *Everything* on dry land that had the breath of life in its nostrils died. *Every* living thing on the face of the earth was wiped out; men and animals and the creatures that move along the ground and the birds of the air were wiped from the earth. *Only* Noah was left and those with him in the ark." --Genesis 7:21-23 (NIV) emphasis added

If the intent of the author was to convey that every living thing died except what was on the ark, what more could be done than this? The fact of what happened was repeated several times in different ways, but each with "every" and "all". This includes "everything on dry land that had the breath of life in its nostrils." In addition to the list of everything that died, we see the positive description of the only things that lived—those in the ark. Again, to claim that the Flood was only local is inconsistent with the death of all of the animals. Some have argued that "all" and "every" do not necessarily mean *all* and *every* as it is possible that it is a hyperbole. However, the repeated iteration and the context are

88

more consistent with a globe-covering flood. Indeed, evidence and arguments against the Flood covering the globe rely on material outside of the Biblical text itself.

Because the Flood wiped out so many living things on earth, the genetic diversity was greatly reduced. Numerous organisms and variations were lost at the time of the Flood as all living creatures today descend from individuals that were aboard the ark. Many creatures went extinct at that time or very soon after as they may not have adapted well to the post Flood environment. The decrease in biodiversity is a consequence and biological impact of the Flood.

A question that often comes up regarding the Flood is: What about the fish? Indeed, there was substantial devastation to underwater environments as evidenced by the abundance of marine fossils. But a bigger issue is the type of water. Since certain fish live in fresh water while others live in salt water, it seems that a global flood would cause acute problems to the fish and other marine organisms. The different physiological systems required for survival in fresh and salty water poses a potential problem for these organisms surviving a global flood. However, at least some fish *are* able to live in both fresh and salt water. Salmon, in particular, spend time in both fresh and salt water. There are also many different types of sharks and stingrays that actually inhabit fresh water environments.[4] In fact, a few of them are obligate freshwater species and will only survive in fresh water. This raises the possibility that many of the marine organisms may have been able to adapt to potential changes in salinity at the time of the Flood.

5. Flood stories from around the globe

Cultures from around the planet have stories and legends that share striking similarities with the Biblical account of Noah. Dr. John Morris of the Institute for Creation Research has collected more than 200 flood related stories from various missionaries, anthropologists and ethnologists.[5] These include legends passed down by people in South America, the Pacific Islands and elsewhere. Almost all of these stories share many common elements to the Biblical account of Noah's Flood. For example,

Dr. Morris shares the following statistics that highlight the similar elements that are present in the flood stories.

Story element	% of stories agree with Bible
Is there a favored family?	88%
Were they forewarned?	66%
Is flood due to wickedness of man?	66%
Is catastrophe only a flood?	95%
Was flood global?	95%
Is survival due to a boat?	70%
Were animals also saved?	67%
Did animals play any part?	73%
Did survivors land on a mountain?	57%
Was the geography local?	82%
Were birds sent out?	35%
Was the rainbow mentioned?	7%
Did survivors offer a sacrifice?	13%
Were specifically eight persons saved?	9%

The striking similarities of key elements found in the Biblical narrative confirm that these points are founded in real historical events. As the people spread out from the Tower of Babel, they would have taken the knowledge of the Flood with them. Thus, the stories would be passed on by word of mouth or written down, being modified in various ways over time. However, many of the most important components persisted. **We can conclude the common elements from traditions around the world are most likely derived from common experience of Noah's Flood as an actual historical event.**

Such confirmation that ancient peoples from around the world knew about Noah's Flood come from the Chinese characters. The character for "ship" or "large boat" is made up of three components: "vessel", "eight", and "mouth" (mouth represents people). In graduate school, a friend of mine from China came to lunch one day very excited. She had always wondered why "ship" was made of those three components. When she read Genesis, it all made sense. The eight people in the vessel were Noah, his wife, his three sons and their three wives *on a very large boat.*

90

Many other Chinese characters reflect aspects of Genesis. This demonstrates that the ancient Chinese people had knowledge of the Flood and creation from before the Tower of Babel dispersal. They went so far as to incorporate these concepts into their language. Although the knowledge was lost, it remains as evidence to us of the fact of Noah's Flood.

boat　　　　**vessel**　　**eight**　　**people**
(mouth)

6. Geological evidence

In addition to the Biblical and historical evidence of a global flood, evidence from the rocks themselves cry out in support. In particular, we see that essentially all of the land on earth was under water in the past. Geology textbooks acknowledge the fact that the continents were all once under water although they extend the time frame over millions of years. Much of the sedimentary rocks found on the continents were formed under water. In addition, we find marine fossils all over the continents including in high mountain ranges.

Besides the evidence for water over the earth, the majority of fossils were formed as a result of catastrophic, rapid burial. As will be discussed later, fossils typically require rapid burial with quick deposition of sediments. This is necessary in order to avoid the normal decay processes which would preclude fossil formation. Another example of the need for rapid burial is the very large dinosaurs which become fossilized. Huge dinosaurs in excess of 80 feet in length, weighing several tons must have been buried quickly. This is expected to require catastrophic and rapid deposition of huge amounts of sediments in order to bury such large creatures. In fact, as the Buddy Davis song says, the "billions of dead things buried in rock layers laid down by water all over the earth" stand in testimony to a globe-covering flood.

Additional geological evidence that supports a world-wide global flood is unconformities. An unconformity is an erosional surface within an area that represents a break in time during sedimentation. The break in time is either due to erosion or non-deposition. They are identified primarily by the difference in rock type or difference in the types of fossils present in the different layers. While the break in sedimentation is clear, the duration of time for the break is in dispute. Evolutionists suggest that there were long periods of time (thousands to millions of years) between successive layers in an unconformity. However, it is also possible that the break in time was only on the order of minutes during a global catastrophe. Creationists support a rapid change in the type of sedimentation as a cause for unconformities. Many unconformities are remarkably flat and smooth which is consistent with a very short break in time. If the break in time was long as the evolutionists believe, we would expect to see erosion, gullies, channels and other types of surfaces forming instead.[6]

An unconformity with smooth contact between Coconino Sandstone (above) and the Hermit Shale (below). The contact zone is marked with arrows. This picture was taken from the Bright Angle Trail in the Grand Canyon. Photo is courtesy of Tom Vail (www.canyonministries.org)

92

Conclusion

The testimony from Scripture, history, fossils and rocks themselves cry out of God's judgment against sin. The fossil record is a record of death, and teaches us about the wages of sin. These should stand as a witness for us that God's judgment and wrath are poured out upon sin. It is ironic that this very evidence of God's holiness and justice has been twisted around into a fossil record of evolution and so called evidence that there is no God.

The fossil record testifies that God destroyed the world once through water because of sin. Next time, it will be destroyed by fire. Just as we can be sure that the world of Noah's day perished through water, we can be certain of Christ's imminent return when the universe and everything in it will be consumed by fire.

Jesus said, "As it was in the days of Noah, so shall it be at the coming of the Son of Man." Just as Noah and his family had to pass through a door to be saved from the ravages of the Flood, so also do we need to pass through a door to be saved from the judgment to come. Jesus also said, "I am the door: by me if any man enter in, he shall be saved, and shall go in and out, and find pasture." John 10:9. Peter says of Noah's ark: "In it only a few people, eight in all, were saved through water, and this water symbolizes baptism that now saves you also—not the removal of dirt from the body but the pledge of a good conscience toward God. It saves you by the resurrection of Jesus Christ, who has gone into heaven and is at God's right hand—with angels, authorities and powers in submission to him." 1 Peter 3:20b-22 (NIV).

---

[1] http://www.reasons.org/about/8_myths_about_rtb.shtml downloaded April 26, 2005.

[2] Answers Magazine had a special issue dedicated to issues related to Noah's ark and the flood with many excellent articles: April-June, 2007.

[3] John Woodmorappe, 1996. *Noah's Ark A Feasibility Study* Institute for Creation Research 1996.

[4] Compagno, L.J.V. and Cook, S.F. 1995. The exploitation and conservation of freshwater elasmobranchs: status of taxa and prospects for the future. *J. Aquaricult. Aquat. Sci* 7:62-90.

[5] John D. Morris, 2001. Why Does Nearly Every Culture Have a Tradition of Global Flood? Institute for Creation Research, *BTG* No.153b.

[6] Tom Vail has several evidences from the Grand Canyon that support a young earth interpretation including unconformities. These can be found at: http://www.canyonministries.com/content/view/31/54/ Downloaded April 28, 2007.

5

Not so Natural Selection

"To suppose that the eye, with all its inimitable contrivances for adjusting the focus to different distances, for admitting different amounts of light, and for the correction of spherical and chromatic aberration, could have been formed by natural selection, seems, I freely confess, absurd in the highest possible degree. Yet reason tells me that if numerous gradations from a perfect and complex eye to one very imperfect and simple, each grade being useful to its possessor, can be shown to exist; if further, the eye does vary ever so slightly, and the variations be inherited, which is certainly the case; and if variation or modification in the organ be ever useful to an animal under changing conditions of life, then the difficulty of believing that a perfect and complex eye could be formed by natural selection, though insuperable by our imagination, can hardly be considered real."

--Charles Darwin
On the Origin of Species

"Ears that hear and eyes that see—the LORD has made them both"

--Proverbs 20:12 (NIV)

Controversy has surrounded Darwin's theory of evolution since its publication in 1859. Indeed, Lady Ashley, a contemporary of Darwin is often quoted as saying: "Let's hope it's not true; but if it is true, let's hope that it does not become widely known." In the

95

United States, laws were introduced in the 1920's that prohibited the teaching of the evolution of man in public schools. Such a law was challenged in the famous Scopes Trial in Dayton, Tennessee. More recently, two court trials *McLean v. Arkansas Board of Education* (1982) and *Edwards v. Aguillard* (1987) were decided by the United States Supreme Court. In the last few years, state and local school boards have considered science standards that included intelligent design or challenges to evolution. Although many scientists and scientific societies claim that there is no controversy among scientists, a small but increasing number of scientists are stating publicly that they are skeptical of Darwinism.[1] Although Darwin's theory *has* become widely known, the controversy surrounding it shows no sign of abating in the near future.

At the time of Darwin and before, one of the dominant views was **essentialism**. According to this idea, developed by Plato, all individuals were only distorted shadows of an ideal or essential form. This view seemed to fit with the Biblical account of creation where God created "kinds" of creatures. People believed that God created the various plants and animals and they have remained *exactly* the same since the beginning of creation. The notion of permanence of form squared well with the view of God as unchanging. Since God does not change, they thought that the perfect forms that God made also did not change. Therefore, the variation that exists was considered a corruption or distortion of those ideal forms created by God.

Such a view may seem quite strange to us. However, we must remember that throughout the 1800's no one knew what the mechanism of heredity was. They had no knowledge of genes or genetics and DNA was unheard of. With no known mechanism or means of conveying hereditary information, it was not unreasonable to propose an "essence" or a "vital force" that was responsible. Obviously, something unseen was behind it and these forces seemed the most likely explanation.

As people began to explore and travel to various parts of the world, they became exposed to a wide diversity of creatures from across the globe. In addition, fossils were found that gave a completely different picture of life. Many of these fossils were of

96

creatures that no longer lived, while others were similar—yet clearly distinct—to modern forms. Extinction and change through time seemed to conflict with the view of God as unchanging. However, this actually confused God with his creation. God can be unchanging and yet create organisms with a range of variation and the ability to adapt to changing conditions. Since we live in a fallen world and indeed one that is cursed with death, extinction of organisms does not mean that God failed or is nonexistent.

Darwin struggled with his observations in nature which seemed to conflict with what he had been taught about creation. As he traveled around the world as a young man on the *H.M.S. Beagle*, he had noticed the similarity *and* differences of organisms on islands compared with those on the mainland. Clearly, there was some type of hereditary relationship between island dwellers with those from the mainland. However, there was no explanation for *why* they were so different. The quest to explain those relationships as well as how new species arise is what led Darwin to formulate his theory of evolution by natural selection.

Charles Darwin
1809-1882

Darwin was greatly influenced by the writings of two men: Charles Lyell and Thomas Malthus. Charles Lyell was a professor of Geology at King's College London and wrote a book titled "Principles of Geology." In it, he popularized James Hutton's view of **uniformitarianism**. According to this idea, the earth was millions of years old and geologic processes took vast periods of time to slowly change the earth. (Uniformitarianism will be discussed in more depth in chapter 8) Thus, Charles Darwin was exposed to the notion that the earth could be millions of years old.

Thomas Malthus' "*Essay on the Principle of Population*" also had a major impact on Darwin. Malthus argued that populations increase exponentially while resources can only increase linearly. This inevitably creates a point of crisis where demand for resources exceeds supply and therefore leads to starvation, death, and disease.[2] Darwin, armed with millions of years from Lyell

97

and a competition for dwindling resources from Malthus, had the two key components necessary to develop his theory.

Principles of Evolution

According to Ernst Mayr, who was described as one of the greatest evolutionary scientists that ever lived, there are five separate components to Darwin's theory of evolution.[3]

1. The non-constancy of species
2. The descent of all organisms from common ancestors
3. The gradualness of evolution
4. The multiplication of species
5. Natural selection

1. Non-constancy of Species

The non-constancy of species is considered to be the main component of Darwin's theory. It is the notion that organisms change through time. Over the generations, individuals are different in a variety of ways from their ancestors. To a limited extent, this is confirmed by observation and is not conflicting with creationist views. Modern creationists view organisms as *basically* the same as their ancestors but not exactly the same. Although we see a wide variety of dogs in the world, none of them have ever given birth to a cat. As will be discussed later, there is certainly a range of variation within a particular kind of organism, but there are limits and boundaries to that variation. This limited change in populations of organisms over time is usually due to changes in the frequency of genes that control those traits. Such changes in gene frequencies and traits through time can sometimes be called "**microevolution**." Microevolution also refers to the changes in gene frequency in a population through time. The fact that populations of organisms change through time does not necessarily help us predict *how* organisms will change or *which* organisms will change. Thus, it has very little predictive power and seems to be more of an observation than a theory.

98

When the Bible says that God made different kinds of creatures, this does not mean that every single species or variety was made from the beginning. In fact, Biblical "kind" is not equivalent to what we have defined as a biological species (besides, the scientific definition of species is not really clear cut.) When we consider that many of the different breeds of dogs have come into existence within the last few hundred years, obviously there is intrinsic or "built in" variation within types of organisms. While God originally made each kind of organism during the creation week, those creatures may have been considerably distinct from our modern species. Indeed, there may even be different "species" today that are part of the same original kind.[4] For example, it is a strong possibility that horses, zebras and donkeys are all descended from an original pair of horses that were on Noah's ark even though they are considered different species today.

Representatives of the horse kind include A) the Mongolian horse; B) the Shetland pony; C) the donkey; and D) the zebra. Horses and zebras can cross as can horses and donkeys and donkeys and zebras. Although horses, zebras and donkeys are considered different species, they are likely from the same created kind.

2. Descent of all Organisms from Common Ancestors

This is perhaps the most contentious aspect of Darwin's theory in regards to the origins controversy. Darwin extrapolated "change through time" over eons of time. In this way, the slight variations observed within a particular type of organism in short periods of time, (horses, bears, dogs, etc.) can be expanded into huge variations over long periods of time. Thus, to the evolutionist, the similarities between humans and apes imply that they shared a common ancestor in the distant past. Extrapolating further back, humans would have an ancestor in common with a kangaroo. Further still, they would expect to find ancestors in common with frogs, fish, mushrooms and trees. Indeed, Darwin believed that all living things were ultimately derived from the same common ancestor. Obviously, a large number of changes would be required over many generations for one type of organism to give rise to another. The process by which the large number of changes that are required for reptiles to evolve into birds for example is sometimes referred to as "**macroevolution**."

When creationists criticize evolution, it is this aspect of the theory that they typically disagree with. While change through time *per se* does not conflict with the Bible the common ancestry of all organisms most certainly does. In Genesis, God made different kinds of creatures and they reproduced "according to their kinds." **Importantly, the variation in organisms is directly observable, whereas common ancestry between diverse types of organisms must be assumed.** Therefore, this aspect of Darwin's theory is not supported by direct observation.

Often the evidence that is used to support common ancestry is the similarities between organisms. Mayr explained:

> "Since all members of a taxon must consist of the descendants of the nearest common ancestor, this common descent can be inferred only by the study of their homologous characters. But how do we determine whether or not the characters of two species are homologous? We say that they are if they conform to the definition of homologous: *A feature in two or more taxa is homologous*

100

when it is derived from the same (or a corresponding) feature of their nearest common ancestor."[5] (Emphasis in original)

Or consider this from a recent biology textbook:

"Similar structures in two or more species are called homologous structures if the structures are similar because they evolved from the same ancestral structure."[6]

Notice the circular reasoning that is being applied here. Common ancestry is inferred by studying homologous (similar) characters and yet homologous characters are defined as being derived from a common ancestor. This becomes extremely problematic and only works *if you assume* that common ancestry is true. The similarity between very different types of organisms (i.e. frogs, dogs and people which all have four limbs) does not really provide evidence that they are related to the same ancestors.

In the same way, the similarities in physiology, metabolism, or even DNA sequences do not really prove common ancestry for different types of organisms. All it does is demonstrate that the DNA is similar. The next obvious question is: What is the reason for the similarity? Creationists maintain that the similarities in organisms are the result of a common Creator. Since all living things were made by God, and made to be in relationship with each other in the same world, there should be similarities. Evolutionists on the other hand insist that it is evidence of common ancestry. It is only evidence of common ancestry *if you assume* that there was no Creator. In the absence of creation, common ancestry is a reasonable explanation for the similarities. However, the data does not rule out or disprove creation and therefore common ancestry remains an unproven assumption.

The appeal to common ancestry provides an alternative interpretive framework for the diversity of life and one that appears to eliminate the need for a Creator God. Unfortunately, many believe that this interpretive framework counts as scientific evidence that the creation view is false. It cannot, however,

101

because evidence interpreted with an assumption (in this case common ancestry) cannot be used to validate that assumption.

3. The Gradualness of Evolution

An important feature of Darwinian evolution is the long periods of time that is required and the slow nature of evolutionary change. In fact, long periods of time are required for the process to work. This is because *populations* not *individuals* are the unit of evolution. As noted previously, microevolution refers to the changes in gene frequency in a population through time. We might consider the percentage of individuals with red hair today compared to 50 years ago. The number has decreased in that time period. Thus, we could say that the human population has evolved—there are relatively fewer individuals with red hair. This type of change takes a significant amount of time because we are dealing with the whole population. Individuals must be born and others die for the gene frequency to change. The process of evolution is said to be gradual because of the time required for the restructuring of a population.

Importantly, since Darwinism requires common ancestry, there must be genetic continuity between organisms. Thus, even though two organisms are distinct, evolution allows no discontinuity between them. Evolution must be a gradual process with transitions or intermediates in between each step. There is no room for any gaps.

4. The Multiplication of Species

Darwin claimed to have developed a theory that would explain the origin of species. Thus, an important aspect of the theory is to account for the vast diversity of life and how all of these different types of creatures came to be. As noted in the opening quote from Darwin, a key assumption is that traits will "vary ever so slightly, and the variations be inherited." In Darwin's day, they had absolutely no idea what the source of variation could be. Without a discrete source and mechanism of variation, they had no

102

conceivable limit to the types or the range of variation that was possible.

Now, we understand that genes provide the mechanism of variability in organisms. Offspring differ from their parents in the mutations that they inherit and more importantly through the shuffling and recombination of the genetic repertoire available from both parents. The number of possible combinations from crossing two individuals is phenomenal. However, it is also limited by the specific genes that the parents have. Although my wife and I both have brown hair, two of our three daughters have red hair. This is possible because my wife and I are carrying genes for red hair even though we are not expressing that trait ourselves. That variation is possible only because some of our ancestors had red hair.

Another way to illustrate this concept is with dog breeding. If we crossed a black Labrador with a yellow one, we would get a "chocolate" one. While the brownish color might appear like new genes in fact it is not. It is simply the result of combining the genes that lead to black coats with the ones that lead to yellow coats. Depending on whether the chocolate Labrador is crossed with a black or a yellow dog will impact the color of the offspring in the next generation. If we crossed the dogs repeatedly we would never get a Dalmatian, a St. Bernard or a German shepherd. The reason is because our Labradors do not have the genes that are necessary to produce any of the other breeds of dogs. If we crossed the Labrador with the German shepherd, we might get some unusual looking dogs. If those offspring were crossed, the next generation might have Labradors and German shepherds in the same litter. This demonstrates the fact that the possible variation of offspring is limited by the gene pool of the parents. The information has to come from somewhere.

Generally speaking there are four major factors that impact the frequency of genes in a population and thus can have an impact on diversity. These are gene flow, genetic drift, mutation, and natural selection:

Gene flow refers to the introduction of new genes into a population through immigration and migration. For example, since the 1600's there has been an influx of genes in North America from Europe, Africa, and Asia. Thus, the frequency of any number of genes is far different today than it was when only Native Americans were on the continent. While this process accounts for regional changes in gene frequency, taken as a whole, it is only redistribution. Gene flow can appear to increase information locally, but for the species as a whole there are no new genes. While novel combinations of genes might arise, there is no real increase in genetic information and no new genes.

Genetic drift is the random change in gene frequencies or the loss of genes or traits in a population. Due to the random nature of gene sorting during reproduction, certain traits can be over or under represented in the next generation. Over several generations, this can have a compounding effect to the extent that particular traits can be completely eliminated from a population. Large populations tend to be more resistant to the effects of drift because random losses are balanced by random gains. In contrast, small populations are greatly impacted. This is especially apparent in islands or other populations with reduced or restricted numbers. While increases in a particular genetic trait may appear to be a gain, it is only at the expense of alternate traits. The tendency for genetic drift is to reduce the variety in a population in favor of a more homogenous one. Genetic drift tends to push the percentage of a particular trait toward 100 or 0 over generations. Genetic drift does not increase genetic information.

Mutations are heritable changes in the genetic instructions found in DNA. (DNA will be discussed more in chapters 10 and 11) Such changes impact when and how much of different proteins will be produced. In addition, they can affect the sequence of amino acids in a protein and thereby alter its shape and potentially its function. Since mutations occur in individuals that are already adapted to their environment, virtually all mutations represent corruptions to the genetic information. Mutations, even if they were deemed beneficial in some cases, actually represent a loss of information because the original sequence has been damaged. Occasionally, a mutation may contribute to a novel trait in an

104

individual such as the Manx cats which lack tails. Such a trait is heritable and passed on to offspring. Although this is a new trait, it still represents a loss of genetic information. Of course, mutations are the evolutionists only hope of generating new genetic information. However, even here the gains are more than offset by a loss.

Natural selection is deemed the primary mechanism of non-random changes in the number of particular traits in a population. Because of the significance of natural selection, it will be discussed more in depth later in this chapter. Darwin suggested that because reproductive capacity can exceed the amount of resources this necessarily generates a "struggle for existence." Individuals with heritable traits that increase survival and reproductive success will pass on those traits to their offspring while those that do not will tend to be eliminated. Thus, natural selection is a culling or weeding out process. It does not create anything new, it only selects from what is present already and does so by a process of elimination.

Therefore, the major factors that influence the frequency of genes and traits in a population do so primarily through negative effects—the loss of genetic information and a decrease in the variation within a population. Most creationists contend that there was tremendous genetic diversity from the beginning of creation. Rather than new types of organisms coming into existence, there has been only loss and extinction.

Evolution is supposed to account for the diversity of life, however, when pressed it does not seem to provide a real explanation. New kinds require new genetic information. As we will see, the only source for new genetic information is mutation which is actually a corruption of genetic information. It is ironic, but the one thing that Darwin did not do in his book *On the Origin of Species* was explain the origin of species.

The Role of Natural Selection

Many view natural selection as Darwin's major insight and contribution; however, he was not the first to propose this idea. The idea actually originated decades earlier with a Christian and creationist named Edward Blyth. Blyth wrote:

> "The same law, therefore, which was intended by Providence to keep up the typical qualities of a species, can be easily converted by man into a means of raising different varieties; but it is also clear that, if man did not keep up these breeds by regulating the sexual intercourse, they would all naturally soon revert to the original type."[7]

Blyth described natural selection in great detail, but described it as a conservative process and not a creative one. Darwin studied Blyth carefully and was well aware of his ideas. In this same article, Blyth describes the "struggle for existence" that takes place in nature especially in regards to animals finding mates. Blyth viewed natural selection as a means for stasis, for organisms to remain essentially the same. This is in contrast to Darwin's application in facilitating the separation and origin of new species.

Darwin tied a number of observations and inferences together into a framework to account for the origin of new species through natural selection:

1. *Each population has a potentially unlimited reproductive capacity.* Left unchecked, every population would increase exponentially.
2. *Available resources are limited.* While the capacity to reproduce is unlimited the resources are not. Whether it is food, space, waste removal, available mates etc., resources are limited. Thus, there is a competition for the available resources.
3. *Each member of a population is unique.* Every individual has a unique genetic make up and set of characteristics. This variation means certain members of a group will have a higher probability of survival than others.

106

4. *Heritability of advantageous traits.* Those individuals with characteristics that provide an advantage when competing for resources necessary for survival or reproduction will be more likely to have offspring which will also have those traits. Thus, environmental conditions will 'select' for particular traits in a population.

Evolutionists readily admit that natural selection is a process of elimination but do not regard it as a strictly random process nor a completely deterministic process. There are elements of both involved. Mayr describes natural selection as a two step process.[8] The first part is the production of variation which is random. The generation of mutations and unique combinations of genes is governed by chance. An additional random factor is which two individuals come together to produce offspring in the first place. The second part is the "Nonrandom aspects of survival and reproduction" which is somewhat deterministic. Given certain environmental constraints, the possession of particular attributes will increase (but not guarantee) survival and reproductive success. Although the survival of an individual is in part due to random events (getting hit by a truck or being at the right place at the right time) having the right combination of genes and traits is supposed to be better "insurance" and thus increases the probability in spite of random events over the long haul.

Thus, the origination of new traits or combinations of traits is a random process. However, for those traits to increase in a population there must be a conferred advantage. If not, the trait would most likely be eliminated by genetic drift.

Evidence for Natural Selection

The most common "proofs" of natural selection fall into three categories: mimicry/camouflage, drug/disease resistance and ability to obtain food.

Mimicry and Camouflage

One of the oldest and strongest examples of natural selection in action is mimicry. It was first described by Henry Bates, a tropical explorer. He noted similarities between palatable and unpalatable species of butterflies across the Amazon. Even in different regions, different types of edible and toxic species appeared to be similar. This effect is called **Batesian mimicry**. It is believed that birds will avoid the palatable butterflies if they resemble toxic or unpalatable ones. Thus, over time, the ones that are like the toxic butterflies will be favored and increase while those that are different will be eaten. Presumably, birds learn to identify the prey that they do *not* want to eat and then avoid things that are like that. However, in this as in other aspects of evolution, there is much more to the story.

In a review article, Mallet and Joron[9] discuss many of the assumptions and difficulties with the standard textbook view of mimicry. The paper begins: "Since their discovery, anti-predator mimicry and warning colors have been used as simple and visually appealing examples of natural selection in action. This simplicity is beguiling, and controversy has often raged behind the textbook examples." Mallet and Joron do not doubt that natural selection takes place in mimicry; however, they insist it is more complicated than is usually provided in the textbooks. They discuss many of the assumptions involved in this type of study including learning vs. forgetting by the predators themselves. The predators have to learn that one pattern is unpalatable and apply it to others. However, time and the number of prey that is eaten can have an impact on whether birds apply that knowledge or not. Scientists are still trying to work out exactly what genes are involved in wing pattern formation as well as exactly what is leading to the types of changes observed.

Even if there is selection going on, it is not the type that demonstrates how birds can arise from reptiles. Change in the wing pattern of butterflies is simply variation within the kind. There is no demonstration of new genetic information. For example, we have no explanation for the origin of butterfly wings in the first place, let alone what leads to the process of converting

108

the caterpillar into a butterfly. Mimicry might lead to changes in gene frequency but it does not lead to new genes.

Perhaps a more famous example of natural selection in action is the peppered moth. Prior to the Industrial Revolution in England, the light colored peppered moth was the most common and the dark variety was quite rare. Following industrialization, pollutants may have killed the light colored lichens, thus exposing the dark bark on trees and the rest of the landscape. The number of dark moths increased significantly compared to the light variety whose percentage decreased. The idea was that lighter moths were more easily found and eaten with darkened backgrounds than the dark variety which was camouflaged. Thus, the dark color would provide a selective advantage and therefore allow those individuals to survive and have more offspring.

In the 1950's a scientist named Kettlewell decided to test this hypothesis. He captured moths, marked them and then released them in different areas. Later, he recaptured them in order to determine what ratio may have been eaten. In polluted or darkened areas, he recovered more dark moths, whereas in less polluted areas, the lighter variety was found in greater abundance. This seemed to confirm the theory. In order to demonstrate that birds were the agent of selection, he placed the different colored moths on tree trunks and then observed which ones the birds would eat. As expected, the birds would primarily eat the dark moths on light trunks but would eat the light moths on dark trunks.

Such an example makes for a wonderful story in a textbook. But of course real life is much more complicated than textbooks. For one thing, there is not just a dark and a light variety. There are very light moths with a few dark specks to very dark moths and everything in between. Kettlewell's experiments demonstrating bird predation were great except for one problem. Moths don't normally rest on tree trunks in the wild.[10] While scientists are still unsure where the peppered moths actually rest most of the time, they are sure that they do not often rest on tree trunks. Since these field studies were done under unnatural conditions, they cannot be considered valid.

In the case of mimicry and camouflage natural selection does appear to play a role but there is one nagging question that has yet

109

to be resolved and is rarely mentioned. If mutations are random, how do the palatable mimics stumble upon the right mutation out of the billions of mutations that are possible? How do the moths or other creatures happen upon a mutation that allows them to be camouflaged? What if instead, it is simply a pre-programmed variation that was being selected? Such a scenario is reasonable because in both cases mentioned, the traits are already present in the population just at low numbers. Perhaps God, in his wisdom provided the genetic variability to ensure that some individuals in a population could survive under changing conditions.

Here is how such a possibility might play out. **Artificial selection** is often raised as a model for natural selection. In artificial selection, a human breeder selects for the desired traits whereas in natural selection environmental constraints are the agent of selection. Through selective breeding, man has generated a number of specific breeds of dogs from an original stock. These breeds can be crossed with each other and crossed with still other breeds to get even more combinations. For example, poodles and Labradors can be crossed to yield a Labradoodle. Perhaps in certain locations in nature, particular combinations of traits are selected for, while other combinations are selected for in different locations. As long as some of the genes remain latent or hidden and there is the possibility of genetic exchange, widespread variation is possible.

In the case of mimicry and camouflage, natural selection, (if in fact it is) only illustrates how there can be changes in gene frequency in a population through time. It is variation within the kind and does nothing whatsoever to explain where butterflies and moths came from. For the evolutionist, mutations and natural selection must e part of the answer to every origins question. As we will see, the limited examples of natural selection in action do not provide answers to ultimate questions of origins.

Drug and Disease Resistance

Another common example of natural selection in action is the resistance to drugs and diseases. In this type of example, the presence of a pesticide or antibiotic kills off all of the members of

110

a population except those few individuals that are resistant for whatever reason. The resistant strain then increases in the population. Two examples that are most often used are DDT resistance in insects and the various types of antibiotic resistant bacteria. The presence of antibiotic resistant bacteria is a serious concern today especially in hospitals. With the widespread use of antibiotics over several decades, there has been a marked increase in the number of resistant bacterial strains. Therefore, antibiotic use has been curtailed especially for those antibiotics for which there is limited resistance. These examples of resistance are often held up as the triumph of evolution. Indeed, evolutionists suggest that creation and intelligent design are dangerous because they ignore this important fact of evolution. Of course this definition of evolution is "change in gene frequency over time" rather than "molecules to man evolution."

While both of these demonstrate that natural selection can impact the gene frequency in a population through time, there are two observations that mitigate their usefulness for evolutionary theory. First, in many cases, resistant individuals are believed to already be present in the population in low numbers. The application of toxin (insecticide or antibiotic) simply allows those individuals to increase relative to the ones that are susceptible. Thus, no new traits are generated. Additionally, some cases of antibiotic resistance result from production of thin mats called biofilms by the bacteria. This protects bacteria from antibiotics even though an individual bacterium may still be susceptible. Second, there is usually a fitness cost associated with resistance.[11] In other words, in the absence of the toxic agent, the resistant strain does not compete favorable with the susceptible one. Without the pesticide or antibiotic, the resistant variety would always remain at very low levels. Further, resistance usually comes with a loss of information. For example, resistance to the antibiotic Ciprofloxacin occurs with the loss of a regulatory protein or a porin (involved in transport of material across the cell membrane.[12] These observations are inconsistent with mutation and natural selection as the mechanism for molecules to man evolution. Evolutionists often blur this distinction and use evidence of the former to support the latter.

111

A related example involves sickle cell anemia. Individuals with sickle cell anemia have a mutation in both of their inherited copies of hemoglobin which is a blood protein that carries oxygen in the blood. The mutation causes this protein to form fibrils and thus alter the shape of red blood cells—causing them to be sickle shaped instead of round. Their bodies destroy these misshaped cells and thus they have few blood cells and become anemic. This disease is most prevalent in Africa, parts of the Middle East and India. There is good but not complete overlap with the prevalence of malaria (Some regions have high levels of sickle cell anemia without a prevalence of malaria and vice versa.)

Scientists believe that the reason for the correlation between sickle cell anemia and malaria is because individuals that have one copy of the mutant gene tend to be resistant to malaria. Although they still get infected, they are more likely to survive their bout with the disease. Thus, the gene is selected for and remains in the population because it is an advantage to have one copy of the gene. When two individuals, each with one copy of the gene, have children, there is a chance that some of those children will inherit two mutant genes. Such individuals do not live long in those parts of the world with poor health care and therefore only infrequently reproduce. Nonetheless, the individuals with one mutant version of the gene survive, reproduce and continue to pass on the mutant gene. This is called a **balanced polymorphism**. There is a balance of different forms of a gene in a population. Without the selective pressure from malaria, the sickle cell gene would be expected to rapidly decline because of dilution of the gene pool combined with elimination of those with two copies of the mutation.

Sickle cell anemia does show evidence of natural selection in action. Nonetheless, we have an example of a loss of information and one that is potentially lethal with two copies of the mutant gene. Such a trait is only selected for because of the high death rate induced by malaria in certain parts of the world. If this is supposed to provide evidence that chimpanzees and humans shared a common ancestor, then it certainly is a giant leap.

The examples given above are repeatedly held up as some of the best evidence of evolution. While it may show natural

112

selection in action, it does not provide evidence of common ancestry nor how all of the different organisms came to be. These are some of the best examples that evolutionists use and yet they fall far short of actually explaining where organisms come from in the first place

Ability to Obtain Food

A common example from a biology textbook on how natural selection contributes to the evolution through the ability to obtain food is the giraffe. The way the story goes is that ancient giraffes had various lengths of neck. As the climate changed, less food was available at low levels. The giraffes that had long necks were able to eat leaves from tall trees while the shorter ones could not. Over time, the short necked giraffes died off, leaving only long necked giraffes to reproduce and pass on genes for long necks to their offspring.[13]

This makes for a wonderful story, even one that Darwin himself elaborated on. The only problem is that it cannot possibly be correct. Giraffes in the wild often eat at shoulder height and below. Additionally, during dry season—when food is the scarcest—is when giraffes are more likely to eat food that is lower.[14] Since I was conditioned to believe that giraffes eat leaves from tall trees I was shocked to visit the Binder Park Zoo. Here, giraffe, zebras, and other animals are in a free range enclosure. Much to my surprise, the giraffe were eating grass with the other animals instead of tree leaves! At another zoo we visited, I did see

Giraffe often eat grass and other low lying vegetation. Here, a giraffe is shown eating grass with a zebra and some gazelles.

113

the giraffe eating leaves high in a tree. Upon closer inspection, however, I noticed that these were actually branches that had been stuffed in a feeder box which was placed high in the tree.

Other theories have been proposed to account for the long neck including heat dissipation and sexual selection, but all of them fall short. Indeed, evolutionary scientists have no satisfactory explanation for the evolutionary process that led to the giraffe's long neck. They are certain it is through natural selection but have no idea what the selective advantage could be.

While there is a competition for food, it is difficult to distinguish between the role of genes and traits vs. the role of luck. In terms of predator/prey relationships it is hard to say that the animal that gets eaten was really genetically less well adapted then the ones that aren't instead of just unlucky. For the predator that is genetically less adapted, is it more likely to die of starvation, disease or attack from others of its own kind?

In the summer of 2006, my wife and I visited Hartwick Pines in central Lower Michigan. This is Michigan's largest remaining virgin white pine forests. As we went through the forest, I was surprised to find patches with numerous maple tree seedlings. These patches occurred where there were small rays of sunlight penetrating the thick upper canopy. At first, it seems that those trees might have had genetic traits that allowed them to produce more food from the available sunlight and thus would be at an advantage and be the ones that would survive to become saplings and then full grown trees. However, it is really more luck as to whether the seed falls in just the right spot so as not to be in the shade. So a tree seed may have better genes but fall in the wrong spot. Besides the limited sunlight available to produce food, there is another limiting factor for maple trees. Deer in the forest eat the leaves off nearly all of the fledgling trees. Better genes won't help a tree survive that!

Also in the Hartwick Pines forest was a tree called the Monarch. This was the oldest and largest tree in the entire forest and was well over 300 years old. The tree died a few years ago. It was struck by lightning. No matter how good the genes are, it is no guarantee of survival. An individual can be genetically ideal

114

and still get run over by a bus. These random occurrences temper the potential of natural selection.

Conclusion

It has been nearly 150 years since Darwin wrote *Origin of Species.* Since that time, the theory of evolution has become the dominant view to explain the origin of species and the diversity of life and even the origin of life. Experimental observations have documented the changes in gene frequencies in populations through time. Scientists have found examples which appear to provide evidence that natural selection can occur throughout nature. These examples generally come with a loss of information rather than a gain or highlight the variation that is already present in a population. Natural selection is not a creative force but one that works through elimination.

Evolutionists often insist that the evidence for evolution is overwhelming. I guess it depends on your definition of "evolution." If you mean "change through time," then I would agree. There is evidence that populations of organisms change through time. But if evolution means "reptiles giving rise to birds" or "chimp/human common ancestry," then I have seen no such evidence. Whether it is changes in beak size of finches or the color of moths, all such evidence simply documents variation intrinsic in populations and the expression of pre-existing (though potentially hidden) genetic information.

The theory of evolution is really a belief system. If you adopt and believe the tenets, such as naturalism and common ancestry, then it might seem to accommodate the data. Indeed, with those assumptions there is no other way to interpret the data. With different assumptions, we can come to different conclusions about the same data. There are limits to the biological change that is possible because God made different kinds of creatures. He provided them with great genetic potential and the ability to adapt to changing environmental conditions. Though some of our modern species (horses and zebras) are likely descended from the same kind, there are gaps between types of animals. I believe that the whole of creation demonstrates the wisdom and love of the

Creator who endowed living things with variation in their gene pool and the means to adapt to changing environmental conditions.

---

[1] Discovery Institute maintains a list of Darwin Doubters at http://www.dissentfromdarwin.org/

[2] Several of Malthus' assumptions have been shown to be invalid. He did not take increases in crop yields or technological advancement into account. In addition, affluence tends to have a negative impact on reproductive rates. There are many more factors involved, some self correcting, that impact the balance between reproduction and resource management.

[3] Ernst Mayr, 2001. *What evolution is* Basic Books. New York ISBN 0-465-04426-3 p 86. While the list of five components of Darwinism is from Mayr, the descriptions and explanations given here are the work of the author of this book. The author's work should not be confused with that of Dr. Mayr who was a firm and committed evolutionist.

[4] The BSG: Creation Biology Study Group is a group of scientists working to understand which organisms make up individual created kinds and what the boundaries between different kinds are. Their website is http://www.bryancore.org/bsg/index.html

[5] Ernst Mayr, 2001. *What evolution is* Basic Books. New York ISBN 0-465-04426-3 p 16

[6] Tobin, A.J. and Dusheck, J. 1998. *Asking About Life* Saunders College Publishing p 315.

[7] Blyth, Edward 1835. "An attempt to classify the 'varieties' of animals with observations on the marked seasonal and other changes which naturally take place in various British species and which do not constitute varieties" *The Magazine of Natural History* 8(1) pp 40-53. It is available online at http://www.bradburyac.mistral.co.uk/blyth1.html

[8] Ernst Mayr, 2001. *What evolution is* Basic Books. New York ISBN 0-465-04426-3 119.

[9] Mallet, J. and Joron M. 1999. Evolution of diversity in warning color and mimicry: polymorphisms, shifting balance and speciation. *Annu. Rev. Ecol. Syst* **30**: 201-233.

[10] Majerus, M. 1998. *Melanism: Evolution in Action.* Oxford University Press, p121.

[11] Anderson, K.L. 2005. Is bacterial resistance to antibiotics an appropriate example of evolutionary change? *Creation Research Society Quarterly* **41**:318-326.

[12] ibid

[13] Tobin, A.J. and Dusheck, J. 1998. *Asking About Life* Saunders College Publishing p 364.

[14] Holdrege, C. "The Giraffe's Short Neck" *In Context* #10 pp14-19 2003 The Nature Institute http://natureinstitute.org/pub/ic/ic10/giraffe.htm

6

You Don't Look a Day over 6,000 Years

"The result, therefore, of our present inquiry is, that we find no vestige of a beginning—no prospect of an end." [1]
James Hutton
Geologist who proposed uniformitarianism

"...I am a young-age creationist because that is my understanding of the Scripture. As I shared with my professors years ago when I was in college, if all the evidence in the universe turns against creationism, I would still be a creationist because that is what the Word of God seems to indicate. Here I must stand." [2]
Kurt Wise,
Paleontologist

Appearance of Age

When I go for walks around the neighborhood with my wife and daughters, sometimes we talk to the neighbors. Up the street lived a kind, elderly man with a unique sense of humor. He would always ask questions like: "Is this the best world you ever lived in?" Of course we answered, "It sure is." If you take such a question seriously, it cannot be answered. Since I have only ever lived in one world, how do I know if this would be the best one or the worst to live in?

117

Likewise, I sometimes hear people make comments about whether a person looks old or young. The comments are a reflection of the perception of an individual and whether they think someone looks older or younger than they should for their age. If someone appears younger than expected for their age, then they are said to look young.

When it comes to the age of the earth, people also make comments about how old it looks. But how would we know? What is the reason for saying that the earth looks old or looks young? There is nothing to compare it to except our preconceived notions of what an old or a young earth *should* be like.

Imagine going to the doctor's office and sitting next to you is a short, frail, balding gentleman with grey hair and dry wrinkled skin. He looks to be in his 80's. Being polite, you ask if he has grandchildren. He has had no children. You ask if he lives alone. He does not. He says he is still living at home with his mother. In fact, she is the one who is seeing the doctor today. Just then a blonde woman in her late forties comes out. He perks up and says, "Ready to go, mom?"

Your mouth drops. This couldn't possibly be his mother! She is much too young to have a son who is so old. That is when you find out the man you are talking to is really a boy who has **progeria**, a disease of accelerated aging. Those with this genetic disorder have a mutation that causes the body to age at a much faster rate than normal. Although the chronological age might be 9-15, individuals with this condition have the physical appearance of the body as well as the degeneration and diseases that usually occur in old age.

Looks can be deceiving.

This problem would be particularly acute if it were possible to travel back in time and be there on the evening of Day 6 of the creation week. In this thought experiment, we would expect to find the world the same in many ways. The plants and animals would be quite different—there would be no cars, roads, computers or cell phones. There are stars and clouds in the sky, full grown trees to give shade, flowers in bloom, full grown animals and of course an adult Adam. The entire world would appear to be quite old and yet it could hardly be any younger. This

118

is often referred to as **"appearance of age**." God made a world that *looked* mature. He did not make Adam and Eve as infants, but full grown adults.

In order for everything in creation to fulfill their purposes, they had to be created fully formed. Since Adam was the first man, he had to be created as an adult since there was no mother to nurse and care for him. The purpose for the stars was to mark the seasons, days, and years. They had to be in place by Day 6 to do the job. Soil would be needed for the plants to grow. There is no deception on God's part—making a world that looks old when it isn't—because God told us how long it took to make in his Word. A mature creation would look old only because of our expectation not because it really was old.

This concept can be confused with several beliefs that are similar. Some people erroneously claim that God planted fossils deliberately to test our faith or to confuse people. In addition, they might suggest that God made the world and all the scientific data such that it would *look* like it evolved. If this were so, it would be disingenuous at best and a boldfaced lie at the worst. It is very inconsistent with the character of God throughout the Scriptures. Others insist that if the earth is young, why did God make it appear so old? Since they do not believe God would lie, the earth must in fact be old just as it appears to them. In both cases, the problem is the assumptions that are being used. In order to avoid confusion, describing creation as "mature and functional" from the beginning may be preferred to "the appearance of age."

Assumptions, assumptions and more assumptions

In the summer of 2006, my family went through a cave in southeast Tennessee. The guide warned us not to touch any of the rocks in the cave because the oils from our fingers would harm the rocks "which take 100 years to grow an inch." Portions of the cave had been renovated and blasted in the 1950's to make an entry way that would allow visitors through. I noticed a very flat ceiling in the opening chamber and one that had obviously been carved out. Along the ceiling there were several straight rows of small

stalactites. These are the icicle-like formations found on the ceilings of caves.

Curious, I asked the guide if that area had been renovated, which it had. I pointed to the stalactites which were about 6-8 inches long and asked if these had formed since the renovation. The guide said, "Oh, no. Those must have been original. They are several inches long and since the cave was renovated 50 years ago that is not enough time for them to grow that long. They must have been there for hundreds of years."

Notice how the assumption (rate of formation) determined how the guide looked at the stalactites. With the assumption that it takes 100 years to grow an inch, the correct conclusion is that those stalactites must have preceded the cave renovation. However, since the cave had in fact been renovated in the 1950's, it is clear that this assumption is not valid. Unfortunately, it is not usually that easy to identify and validate assumptions.

One of the ways to identify assumptions is to keep asking the question, "How do you know that?" At first, there may be good evidential reasons and explanations. The question can be repeated until the answer becomes something like: "I just know." Or "We aren't really sure, but..." Or "I think....' Or "An authority said..." This was the approach that I took with the cave guide. "How do you know that it takes 100 years for the stalactites to grow an inch?" The answer was, "That was what they told us."

I have no doubt that some stalactites take 100 years to grow an inch, but that assumes certain conditions including the flow of water and the concentration of minerals, pH, temperature, and other factors. However, others can form faster or slower under different conditions. This is demonstrated by the tiny stalactites we observed forming on the iron railing in another cave we went through in Pennsylvania.

Assumptions, also called **presuppositions,** are facts that are taken for granted. They help define an interpretive framework and exist *before* an investigation begins. They are prior commitments and serve as a foundation for knowledge. Presuppositions guide our expectations. They cannot be proven, they are simply taken as a given. Assumptions can be shown to be invalid if they lack internal consistency, if they are in conflict with observations in the world, or if they clearly lead to false conclusions. Even then, people don't always abandon their tightly held assumptions because they have *faith* that there is an alternative explanation.

There is nothing wrong or silly with making assumptions, we need to make them to get through life. Generally, people have good reasons for the assumptions that they make. For example, we assume that the bank will give us back the money that we deposit into an account. This is not something that is proven until we actually receive the money. However, we have good reason to believe that we will get the money back. Likewise, we should have some reasons for holding the assumptions that we do.

Creationists have presuppositions too. We believe that God is the Creator, that he has revealed himself and his plan through the Bible, which is without error in the original autographs. Upon those assumptions is built a hermeneutic that allows us to follow the historical-grammatical interpretation of the Bible. Scripture is used to interpret Scripture. The tenets of young earth creationism are built upon this. As has been discussed, both creationism and evolution are built upon unprovable assumptions and must be accepted by faith. Likewise, when we assign an age for the earth and universe, both the creationist and the evolutionist do so in faith.

Rationale for Young Earth Creation

Young earth creationists generally insist that the earth is about 6,000 years old.[3] This date is derived by using the same assumptions as Bishop Ussher:

1. The creation week of Genesis 1 is seven normal ~24 hour days.
2. The ages of the patriarchs given in Genesis 5 and 11 are reasonably accurate.
3. There are no significant gaps in the genealogies of Genesis 5 and 11.

Given these assumptions as a starting point, the logical conclusion is that the earth and everything in it is roughly 6,000 years old. If

121

any of them are significantly off track, then the basis for a young earth would be weakened. Notice that the foundation for a recent creation has nothing to do with scientific data or measurements. It is based primarily on the Bible.

1. The creation week of Genesis 1 is seven normal ~24 hr days.

Several reasons for taking the days of the creation week as normal ~24 hour days were given in chapter 3. The chapter also covered theological and Biblical reasons that millions of years could not precede or follow the Creation Week. Several additional reasons the earth must be young that relate to Genesis 1-3 are given.

- *Man was created <u>at the beginning</u>.* Jesus placed the creation of man at the beginning of creation. [Jesus replied.] "But at the beginning of creation God 'made them male and female.'" Mark 10:6 (NIV) Matthew 19:4 is similar. Thus, there cannot be millions of years between the beginning of creation and Adam and Eve.
- *There was no death for nephesh creatures prior to the Fall of Adam.* It is inconsistent to have animal death and suffering in a creation that God calls "very good." In the Bible, certain creatures are designated as *nephesh* which is often translated as "living creature." Some have rebutted this problem of death before sin by arguing that plants would die when eaten. However, when leaves, seeds and other plant parts are shed by the plant, the plant is still very much alive. Eating fruit would not kill the fruit tree. Cellular death is not the same as the death of the organism. Therefore, this argument regarding plant death does not counter the real problem of animal death before the Fall.
- *There was no predatory hunting prior to the Fall of Adam.* In Genesis 1:29-30, God gives green plants and fruit for food for all land dwelling creatures and birds. Bears and other animals with canine teeth often eat plants. (Pandas eat exclusively plants!) Teeth that are used for eating meat

122

could have been originally designed for eating fleshy fruits and vegetables.

- *The time between Day 6 of the creation week and the Fall of Adam was very short.* The Fall must have happened before Adam and Eve conceived any children. Otherwise, such children would have been conceived without inheriting a sin nature.

- *The purpose of man is to glorify God.* Man reveals God's glory in a unique way through the salvation we have in Christ. The Fall was not a surprise to God but part of his plan. The universe was created for man, not man for the universe. At judgment day, when it is the end of man, it is also the end of the universe (1 Peter 3:7, 10). Therefore, it doesn't make sense to have a universe for billions of years before man exists.

These factors all tie together into a consistent framework regarding the very first few days of creation.

2. The ages of the patriarchs given in Genesis 5 and 11 are reasonably accurate.

One of the more difficult passages in the Bible is the genealogy given in Genesis 5. This is challenging because it lists people that live ~900 years old. (Adam lived 930 and Methuselah 969 years) Such longevity seems unthinkable and many have tried to come up with other explanations. However, such alternatives are unnecessary.

Biologically speaking, it could have been possible for people to live that long. They did not have the accumulated mutations and diseases that we have today. Moreover, if DNA repair, tissue stem cells and other repair mechanisms in the body were working well, there is no biological reason that aging could not be much slower. Consider the example of progeria (the accelerated aging disease mentioned earlier in the chapter. A genetic mutation triggers a much more rapid aging process. Compared to Methuselah, perhaps all of us would be looked on with pity for such rapid aging, although to us it is "normal." Additionally, Abraham's wife

123

was taken to be in Abimalech's harem although she was 90 years old (Genesis 20:1-2). Abraham himself lived to be 175 years old. The consistent long lives and abilities at advanced ages suggest a slower aging process for the patriarchs than humans currently experience. The progressive accumulation of mutations provides a possible biological mechanism for the current "shortened" human life span.

Hebrew scholars generally consider the Masoretic Text to be the most reliable manuscript and it is the primary document used for most Bible translations. Other manuscripts that are consulted include the Septuagint, (LXX) which is a Greek translation of the Hebrew Old Testament, and the Samaritan Pentateuch. A comparison of the ages that are given for the age at "begetting" and the remaining years afterwards shows a fairly close relationship between these various texts. (See Table 1)

Although there are some discrepancies between the ages given for the patriarchs between the three texts, the similarity is quite clear. Notice that while the LXX adds 100 years to the age at begetting for many of the patriarchs compared to the Masoretic Text, this amount is subtracted from the years remaining after "begetting" so that the total lifespan is conserved. As mentioned, the Masoretic Text is believed to be the most accurate as both the LXX and Samaritan Pentateuch show potential signs of editing.[4] For example, the chronology from the LXX would have Methuselah dying several years after the Flood.[5] In contrast, the Masoretic Text chronology has Methuselah dying in the year of the Flood which reinforces its accuracy.

There are potential errors that would arise in using the ages of the patriarchs to arrive at an exact date for creation. First, unless each son was born on his father's birthday, there is up to a year of uncertainty for each patriarch mentioned. Nonetheless, the ages represent a close approximation. Additionally, there is some debate and uncertainty for an exact date of the Exodus from Egypt. Even so, the range of presumed dates for the Exodus does not add thousands of years. Therefore, the ages given should be considered reasonably accurate and give an approximate age for the time frame between Adam and Abraham if we also assume that there are no gaps in these genealogical records.

Chronogenealogies of the Patriarchs according to different textual traditions.[6]

Name	Age when begetting next in line			Remaining years of life		
	LXX	Masoretic Text	Samaritan Pentateuch	LXX	Masoretic Text	Samaritan Pentateuch
Adam	230	130	130	700	800	800
Seth	205	105	105	707	807	807
Enosh	190	90	90	715	815	815
Cainan	170	70	70	740	840	840
Mahalalel	165	65	65	730	830	830
Jared	162	162	62	800	800	785
Enoch	165	65	65	200	300	300
Methuselah	167	187	67	802	782	653
Lamech	188	182	53	565	595	600
Noah	500	500	500	450	450	450
Total (Adam to Flood)	**2242**	**1656**	**1307**			
Shem[1]	100	100	100	500	500	500
Arphaxad	135	35	135	430	403	303
[Cainan][2]	[130]	–	–	[330]	–	–
Shelah	130	30	130	330	403	303
Eber	134	34	134	370	430	270
Peleg	130	30	130	209	209	109
Reu	132	32	132	207	207	107
Serug	130	30	130	200	200	100
Nahor	79	29	79	129	119	69
Terah[3]	70	70	70	135	135	75
Total	**1070**	**290**	**940**			

1   Shem turned 100 two years after the Flood Genesis 11:10.
2   Cainan only appears in the LXX and is a likely addition due to a copy error.
3   Terah was likely 130 when Abraham was born, as Abram was not the firstborn

3. There are no significant gaps in the genealogies of Genesis 5 and 11.

There are three places where people often try to insert long periods of time: *before* the creation week, *during* the creation and *after* the creation week. The major creation compromise theories all try to put vast ages before or during the creation week. Arguments against these were given in Chapter 3. For those who concede to those rebuttals but still want to have millions of years,

125

the only remaining option is to assume that there are gaps in the genealogies. In other words, there are missing people and years which would expand the time between Adam and Abraham.

Perhaps the most common argument is the suggestion that 'begat' can mean "became the ancestor of" and not necessarily that it is a direct father-son relationship. Even if this were correct, it does not provide evidence of significant gaps.[7] Since the age is given for the patriarch when the next individual is born, the range of dates has bookends. So if you say, "Larry 'became the father of' Kathleen at the age of 46" and skip me, you do not need my age when my daughter was born or the age of my father when I was born. The bookend formula means that even if there are people missing, the age still holds and thus the time frame.

Other Biblical genealogies such as that in Matthew skip people. This is held up as evidence that there are people missing from Genesis 5 and 11. Matthew is making the point that there are 14 generations between Abraham and David; David and the exile; and the exile to Jesus. To do so, he leaves some out. There is no similar comment about the number of generations in Genesis. Further, Matthew does not provide a chronology or the ages of the people and instead simply gives a continuous list without historical commentary. Therefore, we find significant differences between the Genesis genealogies and that of Matthew. It is difficult to see the logic in applying a known gap in Matthew (where we know there is a gap by comparison to other Scripture passages) as evidence that there are unknown gaps in Genesis.

Rather than a gap, there is an insertion of a name in the list from the Septuagint (LXX). Cainan is given as the son of Arphaxad and the father of Shelah in the LXX whereas this name is missing from the Masoretic Text and the Samaritan Pentateuch. It is generally accepted that this represents one of the extremely rare copy errors that has occurred in some of the Biblical manuscripts.[8] Note that this does not negatively impact Biblical inerrancy as the Bible is accurate in the original autographs. The evidence that it is a copy error is that this name appears in some but not all of the ancient manuscripts. Moreover, it is fairly clear that it is an *addition* rather than a loss of a name. A name that is added does not qualify as

126

evidence of gaps. Regardless, the addition or loss of one individual would add only 30-35 years.

My father has been working on tracing our family history. He has tracked one of our ancestors back to 1063 which was 30 generations ago. It surprised me to think that 30 generations occur in the span of about 1000 years. What this demonstrates is that hundreds of generations would be required to move the age of the earth back only several thousand years. Vast ages would require huge numbers of generations. If there were hundreds, we might wonder why the Bible mentions Serug and Eber out of the hundreds of generations.

Importantly, Jude 14 says that Enoch was "the seventh from Adam." This means that there is no gap between Adam and Enoch. Methuselah died in the year of the Flood and Lamech (who named his son Noah) died just prior to the Flood. This shows that gaps are not indicated prior to the Flood, when we might expect this to be the most likely period to have gaps. Instead we have additional Biblical evidence to support the continuity and lack of gaps.

Ironically, the attempt is often made to place a long period of time between the Flood and the Tower of Babel or between the Flood and Abraham. Proponents of this view usually make the argument that it is hard to believe that people had fallen into idolatry so quickly if there is only ~300-400 years between the Flood and Abraham. However this ignores several facts:

- Adam's son Cain was a murderer.
- Noah's son Ham who went through the Flood also committed a grave sin.
- The Israelites who went through the Red Sea during the Exodus and saw all of the miracles worshipped a golden calf soon after.
- The Book of the Law was lost in the Temple at the time of King Josiah.

The Bible and history clearly demonstrate how quickly people can lose the knowledge of God and fall into idolatry. This pattern— how quickly people turn away from God—actually argues against

127

vast amounts of time in this period. People do not keep the knowledge of God but have a strong tendency to fall away.

A careful reading of Genesis 11-50 paints a different picture of this period of time than many people typically realize. For example, while there were quite a few people living at the time of Abraham, the actual number was probably very small. It would take time to repopulate the earth after the Flood. God promised Abraham that he would become a great nation. Several of the people who are mentioned in this part of Genesis *did* become nations. We have the various Canaanites, Moabites, Edomites, and so on. For each one, the name of the father of the nation is known. This could only happen if the total number of people in the world was relatively small at that time.

Another example of the relatively small population at the time of Abraham is the story about Abram rescuing Lot. Abram went up against the armies of five Kings in Genesis 14. Interestingly, Abram defeats them with 318 trained men. This is not described as a miraculous deliverance as when Gideon defeated the Midianites with 300 men. It should be considered miraculous for Abraham to go against the armies of five kings with only 318 men and it is presented as a matter of fact. I believe it gives us insight into the relatively low number of people living at the time which suggests it was not long removed from the Flood.

While there is some degree of uncertainty for an exact date for the creation of the world, the Bible is clear that it is within the recent past and not millions or billions of years ago. It is interesting that the only genealogies in the Bible that give ages are the ones that we would need in order to determine an approximate age for the earth. Indeed, if we did not have the ages mentioned for people in Genesis 5 and 11, we would have absolutely no hope of coming close to an appropriate time scale. However, I believe that the purpose of including them is to allow us to establish a time frame for earth history.

I remember as a child hearing Carl Sagan talk about how if the age of the universe were condensed into a year, mankind would appear something like 5 minutes to midnight on December 31. Such comparisons make man out to be insignificant, and it seems to make God farther away. If God made the universe 14.5 billion years ago, then our lifespan doesn't warrant a blip. However, if God made everything just ~6,000 years ago, then this makes God seem a whole lot closer.

Arguments for an Old Earth

Even without any evidence, the theory of evolution requires vast ages for the earth and universe. Since evolution is driven by random mutation and natural selection, long periods of time would be necessary to allow for the production of mutations and after that, to select the individuals with advantageous mutations against the unfit. Evolution and millions of years go together. Whether naturalistic or theistic, evolution requires long periods of time. Many of those who have adopted a creation compromise position as discussed in Chapter 3 use the same evidence for an old earth that the evolutionists do.

There are a few primary assumptions and principles that are used to support an old age paradigm:

1. Light from stars which are millions of light years away from us would take millions of years to get here.
2. Radiometric dating demonstrates that the earth is billions of years old.
3. The fossil record shows an orderly progression consistent with evolutionary theory.

While there are other arguments that have been advanced to demonstrate an ancient earth and universe, these three are by far the most prevalent. Each of these are really based on unproven assumptions and there are potential difficulties and inconsistencies with them.

1. Distant starlight proves the earth is millions of years old.

The stars that we see are very far away. Our own Milky Way galaxy is 100,000 light years across. Recall, a light year is the distance that light will travel in one year. Since light travels at

129

186,000 miles per second, a light year is quite large. The sun is about 93 million miles away from the earth which means it takes 8 minutes for light from the sun to reach the earth. The nearest star to the solar system is about four light years away. Therefore, if that star vanished, we would not see it until four years after the fact. The furthest objects in space are believed to be at least ~14 billion light years away. As scientists study and look at these distant stars and galaxies they often claim that they are 'looking backwards in time.' This is because, if the object is one million light years away, they assume that it took one million years for the light to get to the earth. Thus, the light we see today would have left one million years ago. If the light left the star one million years ago, then obviously the universe *must* be millions of years old.

Such an argument is simple, straightforward and seems difficult to object to. Nonetheless, the argument is based on several assumptions that are not immediately obvious. Some have argued that perhaps the objects really aren't millions of light years away, that they are much closer. Measurements can be made that demonstrate that the stars and galaxies really are millions of light years away so most scientists do not doubt the distances. Assumptions involved in the distant starlight argument include that the speed of light has been constant throughout time and that clocks on earth tick at the same speed as clocks out in deep space.

A popular creationist counter to this argument was that God made the light in transit. In other words, when God made the stars, he also made the beams of light that go from each of the stars to our eyes. While this idea has a lot of appeal, it actually has a serious flaw. Since we have observed **super novas**[9] (a giant explosion when a star blows

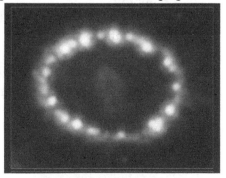

Super nova SN 1987a
Courtesy: NASA

up) which are from stars that are >100,000 light years away, it would mean that God also made the explosion. For the light from

130

the explosion to reach us, it would also have to be made in transit. However, this would seem deceptive because God would be making light for explosions that didn't really happen. Therefore, creationists have begun to seek other explanations for the distant starlight than the light being created in transit.

Another explanation for the distant starlight is that the speed of light was faster in the past than it is now. If the speed of light was faster in the past, this could provide an explanation for how light could get here from millions of years away within only a few thousand years of earth history. This idea of 'c decay' (for decrease in the speed of light which is abbreviated 'c') was first developed and promoted by Barry Setterfield.[10] It was a controversial theory and remains somewhat so today. When it was first proposed, creationists jumped on it as a great solution to the conundrum. Because it received so much criticism and issues were raised that appeared to make it untenable, many began to drop the idea. Setterfield stands by his theory and continues to promote it.

Since Setterfield proposed his theory some very strange behavior for light has been observed. In lab tests, scientists have been able to get light to appear to slow down, stop, and even travel in reverse.[11,12,13] While this is not a confirmation of the hypothesis of decay in the speed of light, it certainly demonstrates that light is strange and there is a lot that we have to learn about it. Additionally, the famous astrophysicist, Paul Davies, published a brief report suggesting that the speed of light was much faster in the past.[14] It was even stated that perhaps the speed of light was "near instantaneous" in the past. Another anomaly involves the Pioneer 10 and 11 space probes. These probes have now gone past the edge of the solar system and have an apparent deceleration. This deceleration is quite unexpected and the implications of this are unknown and will be discussed more in the next chapter. Although this is an unsettled area, it does suggest that we should exercise caution regarding the constancy or decay of the speed of light.

A potentially exciting possibility has been suggested by physicist Russ Humphreys. Spurred on by Setterfield's hypothesis, Humphreys began to think about the possibility of physical constants changing. In Humphreys' book, *Starlight and Time*, he lays out a possible creationist cosmology that would address a number of key issues. Two important components of Humphreys' model are that the universe expanded in the past and that the earth is near (but not exactly at) the center of the universe. Since there are 17 references in the Bible to God "stretching out" the heavens, perhaps the physical space of the universe was in fact expanded in the past. Also, because the earth is near the center of gravity for the universe, this may explain the distant starlight problem.

Gravity has been known to have an effect on the passage of time and this is called **gravitational time dilation**. Although bizarre, time proceeds more slowly when gravity is greater. Thus, an atomic clock at sea level will tick more slowly than the same type of clock on a mountain or in an airplane. The closer the clock is to the center of the earth, the slower the clock will tick. If the earth is near the center of gravity for the universe, then clocks on earth would tick more slowly than clocks out in deep space, further away from the center of gravity. If correct, this would provide a mechanism for light to get here from deep space. On Day 4, the stars would have suddenly appeared, while potentially millions of years occurred in space as the light traveled. In other words, in one day by 'earth standard time" millions of years occurred in deep space because the clocks were ticking at different rates.

2. Radiometric dating proves that the earth is billions of years old.

Radiometric dating is probably the most common argument that is used to support an age of 4.5 billion years for the earth. It refers to a number of different techniques that are all based on the decay of specific radioactive elements. Since the rate of radioactive decay and the number of atoms can be measured, radiometric dating techniques can yield objective and reproducible results. Nonetheless, like all dating techniques, there are a number of assumptions that must hold true if the methods are to be valid. In addition, research by the RATE[15] group with the Institute for Creation Research has shown that there is good reason to doubt the billions of years mandated by radiometric dating techniques.

132

Atoms are the smallest particles of an element that have the properties of that element. Atoms themselves are comprised of even smaller particles including electrons, protons and neutrons. **Electrons** are negatively charged particles that circle around the atomic nucleus. Inside the nucleus, are the positively charged **protons** and the uncharged **neutrons**. The number of protons in an atom determines which of the 92 naturally occurring elements the atom is. If the number of protons in an atom changes, then the atom will convert from one type of element to another. If the number of neutrons in an atom changes, then this can alter the atomic weight.

Radioisotopes are atoms that have a tendency to lose protons and/or neutrons. In the process of radioactive decay, the number of these subatomic particles changes and this converts the atom from one element to another or from one weight to another. When this happens, energy is released in the form of radiation. The radioisotope that decays in this manner is called the parent while the product is called the daughter.

Each radioisotope will decay at a particular rate which is called the **half-life**. The half-life is the amount of time that it takes for *half* of the radioisotope to decay. Interestingly, the half-life of a radioisotope is the same regardless of the amount of material. For example, the half-life for carbon-14 is 5,730 years whether you have one ton or one ounce. After 5,730 years, you will only have half of the original material left. As each half-life passes, you are left with half of the amount that you had before. Thus, the radioisotope decays exponentially.

When using radiometric dating method, scientists might measure the amount of parent and daughter isotopes. Since these values can be determined and the decay rate (half-life) is known, scientists infer an age for the sample. To be valid, three assumptions must hold true:

1. The system must be closed. There can be no gain or loss of either parent or daughter isotope.
2. There was no daughter isotope present in the starting material.
3. The decay rate (half-life) must be constant.

133

In several cases, scientists have been able to devise methods to correct for the gain or loss of isotopes if assumption #1 is not valid. In addition, they focus on methods where assumption #2 can be somewhat certain. Since scientists have not observed changing decay rates, they believe assumption #3 is a certainty. However, it is with this assumption, that the RATE team has identified specific problems.

The RATE scientists believe they have evidence that the decay rates were much faster in the past than they are now. With faster decay rates, parent radioisotopes would be converted into daughter much quicker. Thus, scientists can correctly measure the ratio of parent to daughter and do so with great accuracy. However, when they use the half-life to determine the length of time that has passed for that conversion, they are using a rate that is too slow. This means that the actual measurements of the *amount* of each isotope are correct, but the *inferred time* that passed is not. With a faster rate of decay in the past, the sample would appear much older than it really is. The RATE scientists have a number of different lines of reasoning that point to changes in the decay rate for radioisotopes.

Tiny zircon crystals occur in granite rocks. These zircon crystals contain uranium which will decay into lead with a half-life of 4.5 billion years. The RATE scientists sampled these crystals and found a ratio of uranium to lead that was consistent with billions of years with the standard half-life measurement. However, the scientists also tried a different method to ascertain the age. In the process of decay of uranium into lead, helium is produced. Because helium is chemically inert (it does not form bonds with other atoms), it will eventually escape from the zircon crystal. The rate at which this diffusion happens can be determined under different conditions. The RATE scientists discovered that although it appears that 1.5 billion years of radioactive decay occurred (according to the uranium-lead ratio); the amount of helium remaining in the zircon indicated a date of only 6,000 years!

Thus, by one measure, uranium to lead decay, the crystal is 1.5 billion years old. But by another measure, helium diffusion, the crystal is only 6,000 years old. Unsatisfied with the date of billions of years, the RATE scientists sought a different method. This is another example of how significant a person's worldview is. If they believed the billions of years, the RATE team would not have pressed on to use an alternative method and would assume the first age was correct. Instead, they found a clue that the decay rate was much faster in the past.

A confirmation of a change in decay rate comes from coal and diamonds. As mentioned earlier, carbon 14 has a half life of 5730. Because of that, after 90,000 years (nearly 20 half-lives), the amount of carbon 14 is so small that it is no longer detectable. However, carbon 14 has been found in coal samples scientists had dated at 315 million years using other dating methods. The RATE scientists also found carbon 14 in diamonds which are supposed to have formed billions of years ago. The fact that they can find carbon 14 in these samples calls into question the alleged millions of years. A sample that was really 315 million years old would have no detectable carbon 14 since it should have all decayed long before we could test it. The fact that carbon 14 is present in appreciable amounts provides further evidence of changing decay rates and a young earth.

The important research findings of the RATE scientists have shown that there are viable alternatives to consider in regards to radiometric dating. Clearly, much more investigation should be done in this area to confirm the results and provide an alternative explanation to the conventional interpretation of radiometric dating results. **It also highlights the fact that where scientific evidence appears to contradict the Bible, it is likely that it is our interpretation of the scientific evidence that is in error rather than the Scriptures.**

3. The fossil record shows an orderly progression consistent with evolutionary theory.

Fossils will be discussed in more detail in Chapter 8. They will be dealt with here in regards to the age of the earth.

In the rock record of the geologic column, there is an orderly progression of fossils. Certain types of fossils are found together in particular strata, and they can be used to predict what types of other fossils will be found. The first time that I heard this from a young earth creationist geologist that I trusted, I was flabbergasted. How could this be? My friend explained that this does not mean that evolution is true, nor that the billions of years is correct, nor that there are a chain of intermediate fossils, nor that the Bible is wrong. It simply means that there is an orderly progression of fossils throughout geologic strata.

Evolutionary scientists view the orderly progression and strata formation as taking millions and millions of years. In contrast, creationists view this as taking place very quickly—much of it during or immediately following Noah's Flood. In reality, the evidence that the process took millions of years is the orderly progression itself. For organisms and ecosystems to change, evolutionary scientists assume that vast periods of time would be required. However, different starting assumptions lead to different conclusions. For example, dinosaur fossils and other materials consistent with a warm climate have been found in polar regions. Michael Oard has suggested that instead of the poles being warm, it is more likely that the fossils were transported to these locations during the flood.[16] Thus, the orderly progression of fossils may have explanations beyond the theory of evolution and millions of years.

Perhaps the most exciting discovery for creationists has been the report of dinosaur soft tissue. In 2005, a report in the prestigious journal *Science* documented the presence of unfossilized tissue from a *T. rex* dinosaur.[17] Since these dinosaurs are supposed to have been extinct for at least 65 million years, finding soft tissue was quite a surprise. Indeed, scientists had not ever really looked for soft tissue inside of a fossil bone before most likely because of their presuppositions. The soft tissue was partially mineralized. After the minerals were removed, the tissue was "stretchy" and had the appearance of blood vessels. Subsequent analysis of the material indicated the presence of collagen protein fragments.[18, 19] Interestingly, the amount of protein that could be recovered decreased over time. This means that the amount of protein that they could recover was reduced compared to previous extractions. This suggested that there was

136

degradation of the sample in its current "modern" environment. The fact that such degradation is occurring over very short time scales poses a potential difficulty in explaining how the material could have been preserved for an alleged 68 million years.

The finding of unfossilized dinosaur tissue is a serious blow to millions of years but it is not entirely unique. Recently, scientists have also obtained bone marrow that could contain DNA from fossil frogs and salamanders that were supposed to be 10 million years old.[20] In addition, National Geographic reported on fish "meat" that was supposed to be 380 million years old. They found well preserved soft tissue including muscle, blood vessels and nerves.[21]

Although the dinosaur soft tissue was startling, it has not shaken the belief of many scientists in millions of years. Currently, they have no logical explanation for how such material could last for >65 million years yet they have faith that they will find a solution to the problem. Notice the similarity between this faith and the faith of a creationist—that we will have an explanation for the orderly progression of fossils. In both cases, there is data that is difficult to explain and yet it does not challenge the underlying assumption. Both the evolutionist and the creationist are convinced that a solution will be found that will interpret the data and be consistent with their view on the age of the earth. Which set of assumptions, creationist or evolutionist is correct? Ultimately, it depends on the worldview of the person who makes the decision.

How old is the earth really?

This chapter began with quotes from James Hutton and Kurt Wise, the founder of old age geology and a young earth creationist respectively. Their statements both reflect belief systems and their interpretation of the world rather than factual conclusions based on scientific data. Regardless of the methods used to determine the age of the earth, there are unprovable assumptions involved. Whether you agree or disagree with those assumptions will determine how much you support the conclusions which are based on them.

137

For me as a scientist and a Christian, I prefer to use the assumptions based on Scripture. Science is a fast changing field. In 2006, astronomers voted and decided that Pluto was no longer a planet. Now all of the astronomy books and science textbooks have to be rewritten. Planets are not trivial things. Science always changes as new discoveries call into question things that we thought we knew for decades. Fortunately for us, God's word does not change. "The grass withers and the flowers fall, but the word of our God stands forever." Isaiah 40:8 (NIV)

My friend Dr. David Menton once told me: "If they ever found Noah's Ark, and I could see it myself...if I could walk on all three decks and put my hands on the timbers...if I could see the animal stalls and the feeding system...if I could see all that, it would be the *second* best evidence for me to believe the account of Noah's ark and the Flood. The *best* evidence for me to believe in the Flood is because it is in the Word of God."

In the same way, I do not put my trust in scientific dating methods even if they confirm a young earth. Like Kurt Wise, I am a young earth creationist because that is my understanding of Scripture. I believe the Bible and it is the foundation for all of my assumptions. In a world of change and uncertainty, there is one rock that holds firm and that is the Bible. Though we may be tossed in a sea of doubt and uncertainty, God's Word is a sure anchor and one that can hold us through the storms of life.

---

[1] Hutton, J. 1788. *Theory of the Earth*. Transactions of the Royal Society of Edinburgh 1:304

[2] Wise, K. 2001. chapter in *In six days: Why 50 scientists choose to believe in creation,* Ed. Ashton, J.F. Master Books, Green Forest AR.

[3] Some creationists have argued for a slightly older age and try to extend the time to ~10,000 years. They suggest that more time is needed after the flood and that it is impossible to believe that people would fall into idolatry so quickly after the devastation of the flood. The problem with such an unnecessary argument is that there is no real rationale given for adding 4,000 years (instead of 400 or 40,000 etc.) other than personal preference.

[4] Williams, Pete, 1998. Some remarks preliminary to a biblical chronology *TJ* 12(1):98-106 The article is available at: http://www.answersingenesis.org/home/area/magazines/tj/docs/tjv12n1_chronology.asp

138

[5] Sarfati, J., 2003. Biblical Chronologies *TJ* 17(3):14-18.

[6] This Chronogenealogy was adapted from Sarfati, J., Biblical Chronologies *TJ* 17(3):14-18 2003. The full article is available at: http://www.answersingenesis.org/tj/v17/i3/chronogenealogies.asp

[7] Ham, K. and Pierce, L. 2006. Who begat Whom? Closing the gap in the Genesis genealogies. Answers Magazine Oct-Dec 2006 pp 60-63.

[8] Ibid.

[9] For example SN 1987a is a super nova explosion of a star ~168,000 light years away.

[10] A simplified explanation of Setterfield's hypothesis can be found at http://www.setterfield.org/simplified.html

[11] Scully, M.O. and Zubairy, M.S. 2003. Playing tricks with slow light. *Science* 301(5630): 181-182.

[12] Dolling, G., Knkrich, C., Wegener, M., Soukoulis, C.M., and Linden, S. 2006. Simultaneous negative phase and group velocity of light in a metamaterial. *Science* 312(5775): 892-894.

[13] Gehring, G.M., Schweinsberg, A., Barsi, C., Kostinski, N., and Boyd, R.W. 2006 Observation of backward pulse propagation through a medium with a negative group velocity *Science* 312(5775): 895-897.

[14] Davies, P.C.W., Davis, T.M. and Lineweaver, C.H., 2002. Black holes constrain varying constants, *Nature* 418(6898):602–603.

[15] RATE stands for Radioisotopes and the Age of The Earth. RATE is a team of physical scientists assembled to conduct research on radiometric dating methods.

[16] Oard, M.J., 2006. Polar dinosaur conundrum *Journal of Creation* 20:6-7.

[17] Schweitzer, M.H., Wittmeyer, J.L., Horner, J.R., and Toporski, J.K. 2005. Soft-Tissue Vessels and Cellular Preservation in *Tyrannosaurus rex*. *Science* 307(5717): 1952-1955.

[18] Schweitzer, M.H., Suo, Z., Avci, R., Asara, J.M., Allen, M.A., Arce, F.T., and Horner, J.R. 2007. Analyses of soft tissue from *Tyrannosaurus rex* suggest the presence of protein *Science* 316(5822): 277-280.

[19] Asara, J.M., Schweitzer, M.H., Freimark, L.M., Phillips, M., and Cantley, L.C. 2007. Protein sequences from mastodon and Tyrannosaurus rex revealed by mass spectrometry. *Science* 316(5822): 280-285.

[20] McNamara, M.E., Orr, P.J., Kearns, S.L., Alcala, L., Anadon, P., and Penalver-Molla, E. 2006. High-fidelity organic preservation of bone marrow in ca.10 Ma amphibians. *Geology* 34(8): 641-644. News report from BBC at: http://news.bbc.co.uk/2/hi/science/nature/5214798.stm downloaded April 12, 2007.

[21] Markey, S. 2007 "Fossil Meat Found in 380-million-year-old fish" *National Geographic News* http://news.nationalgeographic.com/news/2007/02/070212-fossil-tissue.html downloaded April 12 2007 The original scientific report was actually very well preserved soft tissue that was mineralized. The fossil was very "high definition"

139

allowing observation under electron microscopy of the tissue structure. Trinajstic, K., Marshall, C., Long, J., and Bifield, K. Exceptional preservation of nerve and muscle tissues in Late Devonian placoderm fish and their evolutionary implications *Biology Letters* **3**(2):197-200.

7

Big Bang or Big Bust

"The Cosmos is all there is, all there ever was, and all there ever will be."

Carl Sagan[1]
Cosmos

"The heavens declare the glory of God; the skies proclaim the work of his hands."

Psalm 19:1 (NIV)

The most fundamental question related to origins is how the universe began. All of the other questions, whether related to the origin of species, the origin of life, or the formation of the solar system presuppose that there is a universe in which to have their origins. This of course is a historical question and thus beyond the reach of empirical science. The origin of the universe necessarily is a one time event that cannot be repeated. The only way to answer the question is to make assumptions, develop models and test those models against observations. Even so, any explanation for the origin of the universe can never be scientifically proven and therefore is ultimately a matter of faith.

A question related to how the universe began is *why* the universe began. Importantly, our answer to the question of why the universe began informs our answer to how. For those who believe in the God of the Bible, the universe has a purpose. The universe declares the glory of God and it exists as a place for man to live. For those who do not believe in God, there is no purpose for the universe and it is simply a happy accident or quirk of fate that intelligent creatures exist who can ponder such questions. If there is a Creator, then there is someone to provide a purpose. Without a Creator, there can be no purpose for the universe.

Those who reject a creation worldview approach questions of origins from a perspective of **naturalism**. Recall that according to naturalism, nature is all there is, much as Carl Sagan described the cosmos. With naturalistic assumptions there are only two alternatives for the universe. Either the universe is eternal and has always existed, or natural laws and processes allowed the universe to create itself. Indeed, both of these ideas have been proposed as solutions to the origin of the universe. The **steady state model** is one that proposes that the universe has always existed. In contrast, the **big bang model** proposes that the universe had a definite beginning albeit one with natural causes.

Both of these models conflict with the Bible. First, the Bible is very clear that the universe had a beginning. God called everything into existence by the power of his word. Therefore, the universe cannot be eternal. Second, it could not create itself. Although some Christians believe that God created the universe by starting the big bang, this too is inconsistent with Scripture. As discussed in Chapter 3, Genesis has plants on earth on Day 3 before the Sun, moon and stars were made on Day 4.

History of Cosmology

Significant advances in our understanding of the universe took place in the sixteenth and seventeenth centuries. In 1514, Nicholaus Copernicus proposed the idea that all of the stars and planets did not circle the earth as previously thought. Instead, he suggested that the earth and the planets revolved around the sun. This was a radical idea at a time when nearly everyone believed that the earth was the center of the universe. Copernicus suggested that the orbits around the earth were circular but this did not fit well with observations. Following Copernicus' lead, Johannes Kepler used very careful measurements and demonstrated that the planetary orbits matched an elliptical pattern around the sun. In

142

1687, Sir Isaac Newton suggested that gravity was the force responsible for holding the planets in their elliptical orbits. These were major achievements of science and laid the groundwork for modern astronomy.

Another major advance came in 1905, when Albert Einstein proposed his special theory of relativity. In it, he suggested that the speed of light was absolute, but time was not. Two events seen by an observer to be simultaneous in one frame of reference moving relative to another frame with constant speed in a straight line may not be seen by an observer to occur simultaneously in the other frame.[2] As a result of the relativity of simultaneity, we cannot define an absolute universal time. This is a very strange concept and counter-intuitive. Our experience of time seems absolute and so this is difficult to grasp. What it means is that the speed of light is the same for all observers. A consequence of special relativity is called the twin paradox. Suppose an astronaut traveled to a star and returned to earth using a powerful rocket ship that could travel at nearly the speed of light. According to relativity, that astronaut would age very slowly during the trip while his twin brother who remained on Earth would age normally. So, the *twins* would have different ages! The special theory of relativity means that the passage of time is observer dependent or relative to the observer's speed. There is no absolute reference frame from which we can measure absolute velocity, position, or time.

Besides the special theory of relativity, Einstein proposed a general theory of relativity. In the general theory of relativity, he suggested that space-time is not flat but curved. Heavy objects warp space-time, and the force of gravity is the result of objects moving through curved space.[3] This too is a difficult concept, but it can be simplified. Space-time can be compared to a rubber sheet. If you place a heavy marble on the rubber sheet, it will stretch the sheet in the middle. There will be a slight depression all around the marble that will then even out as you move away from the marble. One of the predictions of this theory is that light from distant stars would be bent as it passed the sun. This was confirmed during a total eclipse.

143

According to the theory of general relativity, a twin who is at sea level, (close to the center of gravity on earth) would age more slowly relative to a twin who lived in the mountains (further away from the center of gravity on earth.) The effect of gravity on time has been confirmed by experimental observation. Atomic clocks at two different elevations do indeed operate in their own separate time frames although the difference is quite small.

There are three key scientific principles that provide the basis for modern cosmology. Knowing these principles will be helpful to understand how and why scientists developed the big bang theory as well as some of the limitations of that theory. They are:

1. Our solar system and galaxy are not in any "special" or preferred location within the universe. This is an extension of the Copernican Principle that the earth is not stationary at the center of the universe but instead revolves around the sun.
2. The speed of light is constant for all observers while there is no absolute reference frame for time.
3. Gravity is the distortion of space-time and gravity can slow time.

What is the Big Bang?

The Big Bang is a descriptive, secular model to explain how the universe began. According to this model, the entire universe—all the matter and all the energy—were in a single, dimensionless point of essentially infinite density and temperature. For some unknown reason, about 13.7 billion years ago, this point began to expand. As it expanded, it cooled and some of the energy in it formed subatomic particles which then produced atoms and more matter. As the universe continued to expand, it cooled and produced more subatomic particles which formed atoms and ultimately the stars that make up the billions of galaxies in the universe. After stars formed, they were capable of producing some of the heavier atoms through nuclear reactions in their core. The Big Bang is the most widely held naturalistic view of the origin of the universe.

144

There are two major assumptions and two evidences that are used to justify the Big Bang:

Assumptions:
1. Red shifts of galaxies mean the universe is expanding
2. The cosmological principle: there is no preferred location in the universe.

Evidences:
1. Cosmic Background Radiation
2. Elemental abundances

Assumption #1: Red shifts of galaxies mean the universe is expanding

Although most people conceive of the big bang as an explosion, astrophysicists describe it differently. Despite the name of the "Big Bang", there was no explosion and no "bang." Instead, they believe the universe *expanded* rather than *exploded.* Rather than an explosion, the model these scientists use is that of a balloon that is blowing up. Galaxies are presumed to be on the surface of the balloon and as the balloon expands, the galaxies and everything else on the surface expands too. Another important assumption of this model is that there is no center and no edge to the universe, just as there is no unique center or edge on the surface of a balloon.

Scientists began developing the Big Bang model in the early 1900's. In 1924, Edwin Hubble provided observational evidence that raised the possibility that the universe may have undergone expansion. Georges Herni Lemaitre, a Jesuit priest, first conceived of the Big Bang model suggesting the universe came into existence with a big explosion. This model was advanced further when Alexander Friedmann developed mathematical equations that showed that an expanding universe was possible. Thus, the Big Bang was developed as an explanation for Hubble's apparent evidence that the universe had expanded.

Hubble's key observation was the finding that galaxies in the universe are '**red shifted**.' All stars emit a specific pattern of light called a spectrum. Hubble observed that the spectra from different galaxies were shifted toward the red end of the spectrum.

145

Scientists believed that the red shift of light resulted from the same effect that changes the pitch of sound waves depending on motion. The Doppler Effect describes how the pitch of sound from a train whistle changes as a train is moving toward or away from you. As the object producing the sound moves toward you, this compresses the sound waves. In contrast, if the object were moving away, this would stretch them out. In the same way stars that are moving toward an observer would be expected to be blue shifted while those moving away would be red shifted. Interestingly, the farther the galaxies were from the earth, the more red shifted they appeared. Hubble interpreted this to mean that the galaxies were moving away from us and the farther away the galaxies are, the faster they are moving away. Such expansion could be interpreted as inflation from a single point. However, there are other explanations for the expansion of the universe. Just because something is expanding doesn't mean that it was ever a point that popped into existence billions of years ago.

A very strange phenomenon related to red shift is called the Pioneer anomaly. Pioneer 10 and 11 space probes were launched in the 1970's and are now at the far reaches of the solar system. Scientists have observed a blue shift indicative that the space probes are slowing down for an unknown reason. However, after accounting for every possible factor, they have no explanation for the source of the deceleration. They have ruled out a source of gravity because these two probes are on opposite sides of the solar system. Further, there is no similar gravitational impact on the outer planets. Although we have made much progress in our understanding of gravity, space-time, and the speed of light, clearly there is much that we don't understand.

Assumption #2: There is no preferred location in the universe.

A second major assumption of the big bang theory is the **cosmological principle**. The cosmological principle assumes that the universe is homogenous. In other words, the large scale structure of the universe is essentially the same all over. Regardless of where you are in the universe, it is assumed that the universe would look basically similar. An analogy is being in the

146

middle of a dense forest. As you look around in every direction, you see trees. Even though the trees are slightly different and some are closer than others, no matter where you move in the forest, the basic structure is the same. Likewise, the universe looks essentially the same in every direction, and thus appears homogenous. Therefore, scientists believe that the earth is not in a preferred or special location within the universe. If there is a center or an edge to the universe, then this would lead to serious complications for the big bang theory.

In his book, *A Briefer History of Time*, Stephen Hawking noted:

> "At first sight, all this evidence that the universe appears the same whichever direction we look in might seem to suggest there is something distinctive about our place in the universe. In particular, it might seem that if we observe all other galaxies to be moving away from us, then we must be at the center of the universe. There is, however, an alternative explanation: the universe *might* look the same in every direction as seen from any other galaxy too. This as we will see was Friedmann's second assumption.
>
> *"We have no scientific evidence for or against that second assumption.* Centuries ago, the church would have considered the assumption heresy, since church doctrine stated that we do occupy a special place at the center of the universe. But today we believe Friedmann's assumption for almost the opposite reason, a kind of modesty: *we feel it would be most remarkable if the universe looked the same in every direction around us but not around other points in the universe.*"[4] (Emphasis added)

This is an interesting admission. **One of the primary components of big bang cosmology has *no scientific evidence to support it.*** As Hawking admits, there is no evidence for the assumption, it is simply a preferred position—one that sounds pious and humble. If this assumption is not valid, much of the evidence for the big bang goes up in smoke.

It would be remarkable if the earth were in a special part of the universe. It would also suggest that perhaps there is purpose in the

147

universe and a Creator. Maybe that is the real reason for the assumption of no preferred place. **So whether we assume that the earth is in a special part of the universe or that there is no special place in the universe is really a matter of personal preference.** Since some find the concept of a Creator unappealing, they conveniently assume Him away.

Some scientists have noted numerous 'coincidences' regarding the location of the earth and solar system and its convenient location. Jay Richards and Guillermo Gonzalez discuss how special the location of the earth is in their book *The Privileged Planet: How our place in the cosmos is designed for discovery.* They discuss the fact that the earth is just the right distance from the sun to allow for liquid water and life. Just as there is a small range of distances from the sun that would be compatible with life, there are certain regions of the galaxy that are unfavorable to life. The location of the solar system is not in the spiral arms of the Milky Way galaxy but in between—a region called the galactic habitable zone. Richards and Gonzalez noted numerous factors that are required for life to exist and ones which would also allow us to make discoveries about the universe. These line up and thus suggest the earth *is* in a special place and was *uniquely designed* for intelligent life. Since the earth is in a preferred location from the sun and the solar system is in a preferred location in the galaxy, it seems reasonable that the galaxy may be in a preferred location in the universe.

Recently, additional observations have raised the possibility that the earth may in fact be a special place in the universe. If one assumes a random distribution of galaxies in the universe, then there should be a continuous distribution of red shift values. However, this is not the case. Red shift values are 'quantized' and occur in regular intervals. One interpretation has suggested that galaxies are distributed in shells with our galaxy near the center.[5] Such an idea is very intriguing although there can be other explanations.[6] For example, the quantized red shift could result from the 'stretching out' of the heavens during creation.[7] Another possibility is that the speed of light has decreased. If so, we might expect the slowing to yield a red shift.

148

Evidence used to support the big bang theory

1. Cosmic Background Radiation

In 1948, George Gamow argued that if the big bang happened, then it would have left a small amount of background radiation that would have persisted. He determined that this radiation level would have cooled during the expansion to just a few degrees above absolute zero. Later, Penzias and Wilson detected a faint amount of background radiation. Since they picked up the same amount of radiation regardless of where they pointed their detector, this appeared to confirm Gamow's prediction. This radiation is called the **cosmic background radiation** or CMB. The distribution of this radiation is fairly uniform with only slight variation throughout the universe.

Many scientists suggest that the CMB is strong confirmation of the big bang theory and is a demonstration of the predictive power of this model for the origin of the universe. However, confirmed predictions may or may not provide evidence in support of a theory. Just because a prediction is borne out, does not completely validate the theory. Consider the following example:

1. The big bang model predicts the cosmic background radiation.
2. There is cosmic background radiation.
3. Therefore, the big bang occurred.

Compare this with the following:

1. Eating broccoli makes me sick.
2. I am sick.
3. Therefore, I ate broccoli.

So when Gamow predicted that the cosmic background radiation would be just a few degrees above absolute zero, it is not necessarily confirming evidence for the big bang. Just as there could be other reasons for being sick besides eating broccoli, the cosmic background radiation could be caused by a mechanism other than the big bang. A further complication of the story is that the CMB was not really a prediction of the big bang theory. Scientists had already done measurements that suggested the temperature in deep space was a few degrees above absolute zero.[8]

As scientists have examined very slight fluctuations in the cosmic background radiation, they have observed an unexpected pattern. The distribution is aligned with the direction "of the two points on the sky where the projection of Earth's equator on the sky crosses the ecliptic."[9] (The ecliptic is the plane of the earth's orbit around the sun.) While the planets are revolving around the sun, the entire solar system is also moving. It so happens that this motion is oriented in relation to the cosmic background radiation. John Hartnett, a creationist astronomer has suggested that the cosmic background radiation can be interpreted to suggest a galacto-centric universe. This means that our Milky Way galaxy may in fact be near the center of the universe. In addition, a component of the cosmic background radiation is correlated with the solar system. All of this raises the possibility that the earth *is* in a preferred location in the universe which argues strongly against the cosmological principle discussed above.

2. Abundances of light elements

One of the evidences that is supposed to confirm the big bang theory is the amount of light elements (hydrogen, helium, and lithium) that there is in the universe. Scientists presume that only these light elements were formed in the initial stages of the big bang expansion. Of course there are many other elements including oxygen, phosphorous, iron and others. These elements are believed to form only in the interior of stars or during a super nova when a star explodes.

The predicted value for deuterium (an isotope of hydrogen), helium and lithium depends on the density of matter in the early universe. In other words, scientists make assumptions about the density of matter very soon after the big bang expansion and use that assumption to "predict" how much of the light elements there should be in the universe.

There are some additional complications regarding the matter in the universe. First, if this model is correct, then there should be some stars that have only these light elements and none of the heavy ones. This is not the case.[10] All of the stars that scientists have examined do indeed have the heavier elements in them. Second, there is abundance of matter over anti-matter.[11] There is very little anti-matter in the universe. However, experiments have demonstrated that when energy is converted into matter, there is an equal amount of matter and anti-matter produced. Therefore, if the big bang happened as expected, there should be equal amounts. Big Bang proponents have suggested that on extremely rare occasions, only matter is created with no anti-matter counterpart; this supposedly altered the ratio. This is an *ad hoc* explanation.

What the big bang does not explain

The Big Bang is a model for the origin of the universe however it is incomplete in a number of aspects. For example, it does not explain what happened before the Big Bang or what triggered it. There are limitations to the Big Bang model. An educational module from NASA explains:

> "The Big Bang model is not complete. For example, it does not explain why the universe is so uniform on the very largest scales or, indeed why it is so non-uniform on smaller scales, i.e. how stars and galaxies came to be."[12]

> "In its simplest form, the Big Bang theory assumes that matter and radiation are uniformly distributed throughout the universe and that general relativity is universally valid. While this can account for the existence of the cosmic microwave background radiation and explain the origin of the light elements, it does not explain the existence of galaxies and large-scale structure. The solution of the structure problem must be built into the framework of the Big Bang theory."[13]

151

This would suggest that the Big Bang cannot explain the origin of what we really would like most to have explained. Never fear, there are more assumptions that can be made. Some scientists believe that the galaxies and their distribution resulted from slight fluctuations that occurred during the initial stages of the big bang expansion. Presumably topological defects or the results of inflation of the universe itself would account for the fluctuations.

There are even more problems. Scientists have measured the motions of stars and galaxies and can infer their mass based on the velocity. The mass that is inferred for many galaxies is about ten times larger than possible based on the number of stars (and gas and dust). Therefore, they suspect that there is extra mass that they cannot see or measure. This is called "Dark Matter." Another complication is the fact that the galaxies appear to be accelerating. There must be something that has caused the expansion of the universe to accelerate and increase in speed. Scientists have proposed "Dark Energy" to fulfill that role. Exactly what these entities are and if they are real remain to be determined. As more and more problems with Big Bang cosmology are uncovered, scientists propose more and more elements to help keep it together.

A growing number of scientists are having serious doubts about the Big Bang. In May 2004, a group of scientists published an open letter in *New Scientist* protesting the "stranglehold of Big Bang theory on cosmological research and funding." Since being placed on the internet,[14] the statement has garnered over 300 signatures. These are not mainly creationists, but secular scientists such as Hilton Ratcliffe who wrote "the Big Bang explanation of the Universe is scientifically untenable, patently illogical, and without any solid observational support whatsoever..."[15]

To address the growing concerns about the Big Bang model, a number of prominent researchers attended the First Crisis in Cosmology Conference held in Portugal in June 2005. Numerous problems with the assumptions and observational data that disconfirmed the Big Bang theory were discussed. Reporting on the conference, Hilton Ratcliffe wrote:

"Papers presented at the conference by some of the world's leading scientists showed beyond doubt that the weight of scientific evidence clearly indicates that the dominant theory on the origin and density of the Universe is deeply flawed. The implications of this damning consensus are serious indeed, and will in time fundamentally affect not only the direction of many scientific disciplines, but also threaten to change the very way that we do science."[16]

Although these researchers reject the Big Bang theory and do so on scientific grounds, they are searching for other naturalistic explanations for the origin of the universe.

Conclusion

The Big Bang is a model for the origin of this universe that is built on a chain of naturalistic assumptions. Even with that, there are many unanswered questions and problems—yet many people claim that this explains the origin of the universe.

When Carl Sagan said, "The Cosmos is all there is, all there ever was and all there ever will be," he was making a belief statement. It is not a statement of scientific fact or observation but an assumption. There is no experimental evidence that can be provided one way or another. In these respects, it is really no different than "In the beginning, God created the heavens and the earth." In the creationist statement, however, the assumption is that there is a Creator who is capable of making everything. In Sagan's assumption, the cosmos must create itself.

The universe is a mighty big place. Encompassing all of the millions of stars in untold millions of galaxies, the universe extends for trillions and trillions of miles. The heavens declare the glory of God and show how much bigger our God is who set these stars in place. We cannot fathom the vastness of space nor can we fathom the love of God who sent his Son to die and pay the penalty for our sins. Even in this huge universe, God cares for each one of us and the very hairs of our head are numbered. Even though the world is such a big place, God knows us each by name.

As I consider the magnitude of space, I am reminded of the words of Psalm 8:

"O LORD our LORD, how majestic is your name in all the earth! You have set your glory above the heavens.
When I consider your heavens, the work of your fingers, the moon and the stars, which you have set in place, what is man that you are mindful of him, the son of man that you care for him? You made him a little lower than the heavenly beings and crowned him with glory and honor." Psalm 8:1, 3-4 (NIV)

---

[1] Sagan, Carl, 1980. *Cosmos* Carl Sagan Productions Inc. pp4.

[2] A classic example is playing ping pong on a moving train. While the ping pong ball bounces and moves normally for the people playing on the train, to an observer watching the train go by, it would be much different.

[3] Heavy implies gravity and therefore general relativity. The word heavy has no meaning in special relativity. The warping of the space-time is due to gravity. "Matter and energy tell space (and space-time) how to curve. Space tells matter how to move. In particular small objects travel along the straightest possible lines in curved space." John Wheeler

[4] Hawking, Stephen. 2005. *A Briefer History of Time.* Bantam pp 62.

[5] Huphreys, D.R. 2002. Our galaxy is at the centre of the universe, 'quantized' red shifts show, *Journal of Creation* **16**(2):95-104.

[6] Bishard, C. 2006. Quantization of starlight redshift not from Hubble Law, *Journal of Creation* **20**(2):12-14.

[7] There are at least 17 places in Scripture that mention God "stretching out" the heavens. Even the Hebrew word translated "expanse" or "firmament" in Genesis 1 is a word that is used to describe hammering out flattening and stretching gold or other metals. What this means for the fabric of space is not clear.

[8] Sarfati, J. 2004. *Refuting Compromise* Master Books pp155.

[9] Hartnett, John, 2006. CMB Conundrums *Journal of Creation* **20**:10-11.

[10] Lisle, J. 2005. Does the Big Bang fit with the Bible? in *War of the Worldviews* Answers in Genesis pp76.

[11] Hellemans, A., 1998. Putting antimatter on the scales, *Science,* **280**:1526.

[12] http://map.gsfc.nasa.gov/m_uni/uni_101bblimit.html downloaded September 2, 2006.

[13] http://map.gsfc.nasa.gov/m_uni/uni_101structures.html downloaded September 2, 2006.

[14] www.cosmologystatement.org downloaded April 29, 2007.

[15] Ratcliffe, H. 2005. The First Crisis in Cosmology Conference *Progress in Physics* **3**:20-24 2005. http://www.americanantigravity.com/documents/Crisis-in-Cosmology-2005-Ratcliffe.pdf
[16] Ibid

8

The Fossils Tell the Story

". . . [T]he number of intermediate varieties, which have formerly existed on the earth, [must] be truly enormous. Why then is not every geological formation and every stratum full of such intermediate links? Geology assuredly does not reveal any such finely graded organic chain; and this, perhaps, is the most obvious and gravest objection which can be urged against my theory."

Charles Darwin
Origin of Species

"When he came near the place where the road goes down the Mount of Olives, the whole crowd of disciples began joyfully to praise God in loud voices for all the miracles they had seen:
"Blessed is the king who comes in the name of the Lord!"
"Peace in heaven and glory in the highest!"
Some of the Pharisees in the crowd said to Jesus, "Teacher, rebuke your disciples!"
"I tell you," he replied, "if they keep quiet, the stones will cry out."

Luke 19:37-40

The theory of evolution predicts that all living things have descended from common ancestors. If true, all organisms would have a genetic relationship with every other organism. In theory, we would be able to show how all living things on earth could fit on a single genealogical family tree. As discussed in Chapter 5, the descent of all organisms from common ancestors is a key component of the theory of evolution. Although scientists typically assert that common ancestry is a fact, it is not directly observable. On the contrary, common ancestry of all organisms can only be assumed or inferred. The most commonly used evidences for evolution—microevolution/adaptation, similarity and vestigial organs—do not provide the evidence to document this type of evolutionary ancestral relationship between diverse types of organisms. Scientists can observe changes in gene frequencies in populations of organisms, but this does not show how molecules to man evolution happened or even that it happened in the past.

The evidence necessary to support common ancestry must demonstrate the *temporal* and *morphological* progression. In addition, we would expect transitional forms or intermediates along the way. The only potential source of such historical evidence is the fossil record and therefore, the fossil record remains as the single most important evidence to evolutionists. Indeed, Darwin himself acknowledged the need for fossils to support his theory. He admitted that the lack of intermediate fossils was the greatest weakness of his theory. **Fossils** are the remains or traces of organisms that once lived and provide the best hope for supporting common ancestry.

The **evolutionary tree** would look something like this:

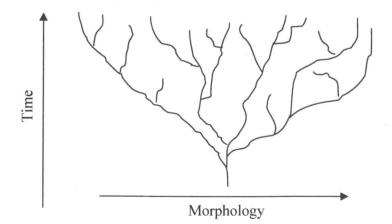

158

A creationist alternative to the evolutionary tree is the **creation orchard**. According to the creation orchard, God made different kinds of organisms with a range of variability. Although there is great diversity within the kind of organism (horse kind, dog kind, and so on), and common ancestry within the kind (horses, zebras, and donkeys), creationists expect no genetic or ancestral link between the different kinds. A creation orchard would look like this:

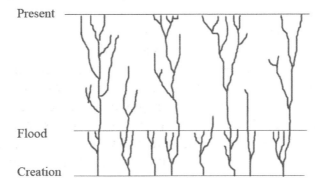

Substantially different predictions for the fossil record would be made using the creation orchard model. First, the creation model predicts sudden appearance of organisms fully formed. God called these creatures to exist from the beginning of creation therefore they would not have genetic precursors. Second, organisms should remain *essentially* the same to the present or go extinct. The unique set of characters and qualities that distinguish them from other kinds of creatures would remain basically (although not exactly) the same. Third, transitional intermediates should generally be absent because they are unnecessary as God created each kind fully formed.

The creation and evolution frameworks provide two distinct and competing hypotheses regarding the history of life on earth. As discussed in Chapter 2, historical questions must be addressed in this way. Observations and inferences can be compared within the two frameworks. The hypothesis that is the strongest, most robust and accommodates the most data is the one that is preferred. It is important to keep in mind that the fossils do not come with instructions or labels. They are interpreted within a framework.

159

How fossils are formed

Fossils are evidence that an organism lived in the past. This is true whether you are an evolutionist and believe in millions of years, or a creationist and only believe in thousands of years. If, for example, we find a fossil of a bird with teeth, then this is convincing evidence that a bird with teeth existed in the past. However, such a fossil does not come with a date stamp that tells when it lived, nor does it come with a family tree. This information must be interpreted based on the relationship between this fossil and others found associated with it. There is a distinction between the evidence of the fossil itself and how it is interpreted. For example, scientists may debate whether *T. rex* was a predator or a scavenger but they would not question whether such a creature lived in the past. Creation scientists would disagree with the time frame and its evolutionary relationship to fish and birds but would not dispute the existence of this dinosaur in the past.

Fossils form in a variety of ways. Generally, most people think about the fossil shells or bones of organisms. These form when an organism is quickly buried under sediments in anoxic (without oxygen) conditions. Typically, when an organism dies, the normal decay process and exposure to the elements will prevent fossil formation. Therefore, rapid burial is a requirement for the formation of a fossil. **Trace fossils** refer to the footprints, tunnels and tracks that are left by animals. Insects and other organisms can become trapped in tree resin called **amber**. The insects become stuck in the gooey resin which then hardens, preserving the insect. **Body fossils** are formed from the mineralization of the hard parts of an organism such as bone, shells, and teeth. Plants and soft bodied organisms can occasionally form fossils too. **Imprints** are impressions from bones or other types of tissue. In almost all cases, the material must be buried rapidly in order for fossils to be preserved. Another type of fossil is a **coprolite** which is fossilized dung. Such fossils are extremely important because they can contain material that can shed light on an organism's diet.

Fossils can convey a great deal of information and shed light on the world of the past. For example, scientists have found fossil

160

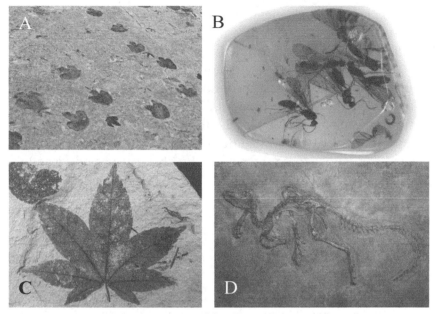

Representatives of various types of fossils. A) Dinosaur footprints are an example of trace fossils. B) Wasps trapped in amber. C) Soft tissues such as a leaf can form fossils. D) Typical example of preserved body parts shown in this dinosaur fossil.

nests which can provide information about reproduction and lifestyle of an organism. Footprints and tracks can yield information about locomotion and speed of an organism. Sometimes fossil material from the region of the gut can provide information on diet.

There are also serious limitations to the study of fossils. Since most fossils are restricted to bones and other hard parts, information regarding soft organ tissue as well as physiology and aspects of behavior can often only be inferred. Further, the actual material from fossils is often fragmentary. An entire skeleton is quite rare and therefore the complete anatomy of some creatures remains elusive. Also, the fossil record does not provide a representative sample of organisms. Marine invertebrates comprise a disproportionately large potion of the fossil record while terrestrial vertebrates comprise relatively few. This is because the conditions required for fossil formation favor marine creatures and tend to particularly exclude forest animals.

Fossils have helped scientists discover much about the past and organisms that no longer live on earth. However, there is much that cannot be discerned from the fossil record. For example, scientists can reconstruct communities based on the types and combinations of fossils that are found. But they cannot be certain that those are the only members of that particular ecosystem and location. It is also possible that the fossil remains were transported to their current location. In addition, new fossils are found all the time and sometimes these finds radically change our understanding of the past.

Interpreting Fossils

A very perplexing problem from a creationist perspective is the consistent pattern of fossils in the rock record. Certain combinations of organisms are found as fossils in particular strata and in progressive layers. For example, dinosaur fossils are associated with gymnosperm plants but not many angiosperms (flowering plants.) Evolutionists have interpreted this as a succession of communities with mass extinction taking place in between the different types. Creationists have always held that most of the fossils were likely produced during the Flood. However, the early expectation was that a global flood would have caused the organisms to be jumbled up and therefore we would not have an ordered progression. In addition, there are tracks that can be found in various types of strata. Other strange features are the cases where hundreds of one type of organism are found together. This would seem unlikely during a global catastrophe.

Evolutionists have typically interpreted the fossil record to show a series of mass extinctions. They see a diversity of organisms in particular strata and then a different set of organisms above those. Indeed, many of the organisms present in lower layers are missing from the upper layers. This is interpreted as extinction, followed by diversification and subsequent extinctions again. According to evolutionists, these represent a temporal sequence of vast amounts of time. The apparent progression and extinction pattern presents a potential difficulty for creationists.

Recently, creationists have proposed a possible solution to the ordered progression of fossils that remains consistent with a key fact of Biblical creation. If God made all things during six days of creation, then all of the kinds of organisms should be contemporaries.[1] However, just because the animals and plants may have been alive at the same time does not mean that they would necessarily all live in the same location.

In *Faith, Form and Time*, paleontologist Kurt Wise describes a variety of possible ecosystems that may have existed on earth. There may have been distinct ecological zones just like we see today (desert, forest, jungle, swamp, etc.) except there were several diverse types which are no longer present on earth. One example are "floating forests" which are believed to have been extensive forests with many types of organisms on a huge floating mat. The tree and other plant roots may have been intertwined in a manner similar to a bog. Dense mats of this type may have provided necessary shelter and habitat for unique organisms. After the Flood, such forests could not reform and thus organisms that were dependent on such an environment could not survive. Another example was a dinosaur/gymnosperm habitat. In this area, mammals and flowering plants were generally absent. An explanation for these different types of fossils being found in different layers is they may have been at different altitudes. Thus, the vertical position of fossils may not represent differences in time but rather their ecological and vertical position on the surface of the earth. There are potential alternative explanations that creationist researchers are exploring.

The make-up of the pre-Flood world has been severely masked by the devastation and death that followed the Flood. Obviously there was a much greater diversity of organisms and ecosystems in the past. But exactly what they looked like will remain a mystery. Evolutionists argue that the fossil record documents a temporal sequence spanning millions of years. But there are alternatives that could be consistent with a creationist perspective.

History of Thought in Geology

The stage for compromise on creation and the age of the earth was set decades before Charles Darwin wrote *Origin of Species*.[2] During the Enlightenment of the 17th and 18th centuries, human reason became the supreme authority even over the Scriptures. Also at this time was the rise of Deism and natural theology. According to Deism, God was impersonal and not involved in sustaining the creation. Instead, he simply created the universe and then let it run according to the laws that he set up from the beginning. Deists rejected miracles and any intervention or involvement of God in the world besides getting the ball rolling at the beginning. Natural theology was the study of nature in order to reveal truths about God. The main premise was that God could be known through the study of his creation. Both of these philosophies took a dim view of revealed truth as found in the Bible. The diminished respect for the Word of God opened a door to compromise that has swung far wider in the years since.

An example of how Deism impacted geology is the work of Abraham Werner (1749-1817). Werner was an extremely influential geologist from Germany. He proposed that the earth was initially covered by a hot, steamy ocean full of dissolved minerals. This ocean cooled and then the minerals formed the sedimentary rocks. Such a theory was totally inconsistent with the Biblical account, but as a Deist, Werner was not obligated to pay any attention to it. Werner had many students while teaching at the University of Freiberg for 40 years. He taught them all that the earth was ancient and emphasized that the rocks were more reliable than any written document for discerning earth history. Thus, from the early days in the history of geology, many people were taught to disregard Genesis.

James Hutton also had a view of earth history that was completely at odds with the Bible. Hutton viewed earth as continuously cycling over and over again. He saw that water eroded the surface of the earth, carrying the sediment to the ocean. Once there, the sediment compacted into rocks and then the forces of heat and pressure would cause them to form new land. Hutton believed this was a continuous and endless process and that there

164

had been a "succession of former worlds." This led him to write his famous phrase "no vestige of a beginning, no prospect of an end." Such a view of earth history is called **uniformitarianism**. It is often defined as "the present is the key to the past" and is used to describe the process of geologic change over long periods of time. Hutton's cyclic view of earth history was a product of his Deistic beliefs and expectation that the rock cycle was governed by natural law.[3]

Hutton's ideas of uniformitarianism were promoted by John Playfair and Charles Lyell. Playfair was a mathematician and clergyman yet argued along with Hutton that the earth was quite ancient. Because Playfair was a much better and more persuasive writer than Hutton, many of the early geologists used Playfair's 1802 book, *Illustrations of the Huttonian Theory of the Earth,* instead of Hutton's own writings. In 1830, Lyell published the first volume of *Principles of Geology* in which he advocated an even stronger form of uniformitarianism Lyell suggested that the rates and intensity of geologic processes proceeded consistently through time. Thus, to determine the length of time required to carve out a canyon, one would need only measure the depth of the canyon and divide by the rate of erosion in the present. The application of uniform rates was an amplification of Hutton's uniformitarianism.

In contrast to uniformitarianism, some viewed the earth as passing through a series of global catastrophes. This view is called **catastrophism**. The uniformitarian view was opposed by catastrophists such as Baron Georges Cuvier. Cuvier was a French anatomist who also studied fossil organisms. Cuvier confirmed the observations that there is a regular progression of types of fossils in strata. He also saw how the types of fossils could change greatly from strata to strata. For example, the fossils in one stratum could be significantly different from those found immediately above it. Cuvier believed that these represented a series of global catastrophes. Moreover, with each catastrophe, virtually all life was wiped out and then the earth was repopulated. Interestingly, Cuvier thought the most recent catastrophe was a flood about 5,000 years ago. Cuvier too, ignored the account of Creation in Genesis. The catastrophists and the uniformitarians debated vigorously about which provided the best explanation for earth history. Although some geologists held to catastrophism, their influence waned considerably after Lyell and thus most geologists adopted uniformitarianism and millions of years for earth history.

William Smith was a British canal builder. He had studied fossils in the various strata that were exposed by canal and road cuts. Smith proposed that the types of fossils could be used to correlate strata in different regions. If these strata contained the same types of fossils, then they would be considered to have been deposited at the same time. Correlating fossils and strata in this way is called **stratigraphy**. Stratigraphy covers the relationships of sedimentary rocks. Correlations can be done either by time (via fossils) or by physical attributes of the strata (same type of rock.) Such correlations of strata by the fossils they contain could be done over short or large distances. This led to the **principle of biologic succession**. Since differences in the animal and plant remains differed in successive sedimentary rock units, it was argued that those communities existed at particular times. According to this idea, the organisms that lived during different time periods were unique. Therefore, paleontologists could use those fossils to determine contemporary deposits and assemble the fossils into a chronological sequence. Of course this assumes that the different types of fossils are only separated by the time period. There may well be many other factors that are involved. As in many of the other areas we have considered, here too, the assumptions that are used to interpret data are extremely significant.

It was not only scientists who had abandoned Scripture and adopted millions of years of history. Several prominent theologians in the early 1800s' contributed to the rejection of traditional views of creation.[4] Thomas Chalmers was a pastor from Scotland who first promoted the gap theory in 1804. A bishop named John Bird Sumner and E.B. Pusey, an Old Testament Professor at Oxford both promoted the gap theory (See Chapter 3 for a discussion of the gap theory.) Others such as Stanley Faber and Hugh Miller began to promote the day-age theory. Thus, compromise on Genesis was taking place

166

simultaneously with the promotion of long periods of time as geology was being formed as a scientific discipline.

However, some geologists and clergy together argued vehemently against such old earth compromises. These men have been collectively called 'Scriptural geologists' because of their high regard for the Bible and insistence that geology be interpreted from within a Biblical framework. They raised both theological and scientific objections to the old earth interpretations of both the catastrophists and the uniformitarians. They maintained both that the earth was young and Noah's flood was global in extent and effect.

One such Scriptural geologist was Granville Penn. Although only an amateur geologist, Penn argued persuasively against those who suggested God had created the world over eons of time— spending a long time getting the planet ready for mankind to live on it. Part of Penn's argument was that it was preposterous to suppose that God would create through a long perfecting process when he could just have easily created it perfect in the first place. He wrote:

> "The vast length of time, which this sinistrous choice is necessarily obliged to call in for its own defense, could only be requisite to the Creator for overcoming difficulties obstructing the perfecting process; it therefore chooses to suppose, that He created obstructions in matter, to resist and retard the perfecting of the work which He designed; whilst at the same time he might have perfected it without any resistance at all, by His own Creative act...To suppose then, a priori, and without the slightest motive prompted by reason, that His wisdom willed, at the same time, both the formation of a perfect work, and a series of resistances to obstruct and delay that perfect work, argues a gross defect of intelligence somewhere; either in the Creator or in the supposer; and I leave it to this science, to determine the alternative."[5]

Penn saw that it made no sense to suggest that God would create over long periods of time because it would be unnecessary for him

167

to do so. If it were, it would only be to overcome obstacles that he had set up himself.

Features of the Fossil Record

As mentioned in the beginning of this chapter, the evolution and creation models make different predictions regarding the fossil record. According to the evolution framework, we should expect to find a progression of fossils of increasing complexity. In addition, we should expect to find transitional intermediates along the way. On the other hand, the creation model suggests sudden appearance of fully formed organisms with an overall lack of transitional intermediates. Since the fossils themselves are silent about their ancestry, it is up to scientists to interpret the evidence. This evidence will be interpreted within the framework of the investigator.

Probably one of the most famous quotes regarding the fossil record is that of the late Stephen J. Gould. Gould was an outstanding paleontologist and professor at Harvard University, who was willing to take a creationist, (Kurt Wise) as a student. Although a staunch evolutionist, his observations on the fossil record had often been used by creationists, much to his chagrin. One of the major tenets of Neo-Darwinian evolution was **gradualism**—that morphological change in organisms should be extremely slow throughout time. However, Gould saw evidence of what he considered rapid change. It was this sudden appearance of fully formed organisms without transitional intermediates that led Gould and Eldridge to propose their theory of punctuated equilibrium.

Regarding the fossil record Gould wrote:

> "The history of most fossil species includes two features particularly inconsistent with gradualism: 1. Stasis. Most species exhibit no directional change during their tenure on earth. They appear in the fossil record looking much the same as when they disappear; morphological change is usually limited and directionless. 2. Sudden appearance. In any local area, a species does not arise gradually by the

168

steady transformation of its ancestors; it appears all at once and 'fully formed.'"[6]

To his dying day, Gould did not express doubts about evolution and the quote used here should not suggest otherwise. He argued strongly against gradualism—the slow steady change of organisms through time—not against evolution per se. Since creationists used this quote so much against him and against evolution, the usual charge is that creationists are taking the quote out of context. Therefore, I want to go out of my way to say that in context: **Gould argued against gradualism and not evolution itself.** However, Gould was stating facts. The facts, based on the fossils, are that most species exhibit no directional change and when they appear in the fossil record they appear fully formed.

In another place, Gould emphasizes a similar contention:

> "The extreme rarity of transitional forms in the fossil record persists as the trade secret of paleontology. The evolutionary trees that adorn our textbooks have data only at the tips and nodes of their branches; the rest is inference, however reasonable, not the evidence of fossils.[7]

Again, for clarity, Gould is arguing against gradualism not evolution itself. Further, Gould did not say that transitional forms are completely absent only that they are rare. Gould used this information to argue in favor of what he and fellow paleontologist Niles Eldridge called **punctuated equilibrium**. According to the theory of punctuated equilibrium, populations of organisms go long periods of time with **stasis**, where they remain essentially the same. Then a portion of the population has a short period of rapid change. Thus, they claimed that the reason that the transitional intermediates are not observed in the fossil record is because the transitional intermediates were few in number and short lived relative to the other forms. In contrast, Neo-Darwinian gradualism postulated long periods of evolution usually within the entire species or population.

Gould was not the only one to acknowledge these features of the fossil record. Ernst Mayr, whom Gould described as "The world's greatest living evolutionary biologist and a writer of extraordinary insight and clarity,"[8] had similar comments.

> "The reason why this controversy has not been fully settled is because there seems to be an astonishing conflict between theory and observation. According to Darwinian theory, evolution is a populational phenomenon and should therefore be gradual and continuous. This should be true not only for microevolution but also for macroevolution and for the transition between the two. Alas, this seems to be in conflict with observation. Wherever we look at the living biota, whether at the level of the higher taxa or even at that of the species, discontinuities are overwhelmingly frequent. Among living taxa there is no intermediacy between whales and terrestrial mammals, nor between reptiles and either birds or mammals. All 30 phyla of animals are separated from each other by a gap. There seems to be a large gap between the flowering plants (angiosperms) and their nearest relatives. *The discontinuities are even more striking in the fossil record. New species usually appear in the fossil record suddenly, not connected with their ancestors by a series of intermediates.* Indeed there are rather few cases of continuous series of gradually evolving species."[9] (Emphasis added)

Mayr also wrote:

> "Given the fact of evolution, one would expect the fossils to document a gradual steady change from ancestral forms to the descendants. But this is not what the paleontologist finds. Instead, he or she finds gaps in just about every phyletic series. New types often appear quite suddenly, and their immediate ancestors are absent in the earlier geological strata. The discovery of unbroken series of species changing gradually into descending species is very rare. Indeed the fossil record is one of discontinuities, seemingly documenting jumps (*saltations*) from one type

170

of organism to a different type. This raises a puzzling question: Why does the fossil record fail to reflect the gradual change one would expect from evolution."[10]

Mayr fully supported evolution and had no doubt about it. Nonetheless, he also acknowledged the overall lack of intermediates and sudden appearance. Mayr's explanation for these features of the fossil record was simply "an artifact of the haphazard history of the preservation and recovery of fossils."[11] This is a typical response from evolutionists.

Both Mayr and Gould recognized these important features of the fossil record: sudden appearance, stasis, and discontinuities. However each of them had slightly different explanations as to why the data is the way that it is. Creationists have another explanation. These features are all real and not simply artifacts of an imperfect process. The reason that transitional intermediates are not found in the fossil record is because they never existed. In reality, it is impossible to discern which of these explanations is correct using the scientific method. It depends on the weight an individual places on various types of evidences.

Transitional Intermediates

According to the creation model, God created different kinds of plants and animals. He blessed them and called them to "reproduce after their kind." Although we do not know exactly what the limit of the Biblical 'kind' was, it clearly shows that there are boundaries or gaps between different types of organisms. For example, we believe that all of the different types of dog breeds as well as wolves, coyotes, foxes and dingoes all share a common ancestor. However, that does not mean that dogs, horses and cats all had an ancestor in common. Evolutionists claim that they did. The evidence for this would necessarily be transitional intermediates. In other words, if such common ancestors existed, we should be able to find at least some of them.

As Gould and Mayr pointed out, such transitional intermediates are rare. However, whether or not one finds transitions depends in part on the definition of a transitional intermediate. The human brain has an enormous capacity to fill in gaps and find relationships. Just as we might assume that a motorcycle is a "transitional intermediate" between a bicycle and an automobile, we could identify a fossil that had characteristics common to two types of creatures and assume that it was an intermediate. For example, *Archaeopteryx* is an alleged transition between reptiles and birds. It has teeth, a claw on its wing, and a bony tail. Yet, it has feathers and a bird brain with a large cerebellum. In one sense, such a combination of traits is suggestive of a common ancestor. Nonetheless, the

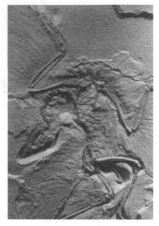

Archaeopteryx

combination itself does not prove the animal is an intermediate because it could have been separately created and endowed with a unique set of characteristics. Indeed, other fossil birds also had teeth. A modern bird called the hoatzin makes use of a wing claw. So there are organisms that have intermediate or combinations of characters but may not necessarily be transitional intermediates. They may be intermediate in form, but not due to common ancestry.

Books on evolution commonly portray what is called an evolutionary tree. In these diagrams, they will place organisms on different branches of an evolutionary tree. Importantly, the dashed

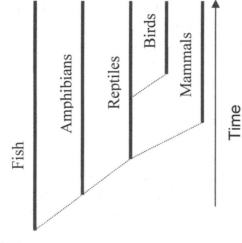

A typical evolutionary tree diagram indicates the alleged ancestral relationships. Dashed lines link various groups.

Dashed lines indicate a presumed evolutionary relationship but one for which fossil evidence is lacking.

172

lines show *presumed* evolutionary relationships. According to the evolution model, there should be transitional intermediates between each class of vertebrate. However, these are precisely the transitional forms that are missing. Even though there are fossils of what are called "mammal like reptiles," these are not necessarily true transitional intermediates. The problem is it cannot be demonstrated that the animals with combinations of reptile and mammal characteristics are in fact a genealogical intermediates and not ones that were separately created.

In many cases, it is difficult to envision how intermediate forms could have bridged significant differences in form. Some of the necessary transitions are very problematic. For example, amphibians live part of their lives in water and indeed must stay moist. If they do not stay moist, they will literally dry up and die as they carry out significant gas exchange through their skin. Reptiles, on the other hand, will not dry out. Amphibians typically lay eggs in water with a jelly coating whereas reptiles lay amniotic eggs with a hard outer shell. These are significant modifications among a host of others which would be necessary for amphibians to "give rise to" reptiles. These would require genetic mutations that would convey a selective advantage such that those individuals which possessed them would increase in proportion relative to those that did not.

Conclusion

Evolutionists count on the fossil record for their strongest evidence for evolution. However, even with millions of fossils that have been found, they acknowledge that the fossils they have yet to find are the very fossils that would prove their case. The major features of the fossil record are stasis and sudden appearance both of which are predictions of the creation model. Although the fossil record does show a pattern and distribution of types of organisms, these do not necessarily represent changes through time. Creationists are currently developing alternative models to account for the distribution of the fossils while maintaining a framework where all of the different types are contemporaries consistent with a literal 6-Day creation.

The fossils tell the story. The fossils show evidence of sudden appearance, of organisms remaining the same and an overall lack of transitional intermediates. These are consistent with a creation model. Jesus said, "If they keep quiet, the stones will cry out." So indeed, the rocks and fossils do cry out in testimony of the Creator of the universe. However, in order to hear this story from the rocks and fossils, one must be willing to listen.

---

[1] This does not mean that each and every species or breed has been contemporaries. For example, some breeds of dogs have only been around for a few hundred years and the same is true for some horse breeds. So specific breeds may not have been living at the same time, but the kinds have.

[2] An excellent book on the history of old earth compromise and geology is Mortenson, Terry 2004. *The Great Turning Point* Master Books. Dr. Mortenson documents clearly the role of the Scriptural geologists.

[3] Ibid pp29

[4] Ibid pp33-36

[5] Penn, Comparative Estimate, I: p 124-127 as quoted in Mortenson, Terry 2004. *The Great Turning Point* Master Books. pp 69.

[6] Gould, Stephen J. 1980. *The Panda's Thumb* pp181-182

[7] Gould, Stephen J. 1987. "Evolution's Erratic Pace" *Natural History* 86:14.

[8] Ernst Mayr, 2001. *What evolution is* Basic Books. New York ISBN 0-465-04426-3 book jacket quote by Stephen Jay Gould Basic Books.

[9] Mayr, Ernst, 2001. *What evolution is* Basic Books. New York ISBN 0-465-04426-3 pp 189.

[10] Ibid pp14

[11] Ibid pp 191

9

Image of God or Planet of Apes

"A rat is a pig is a dog is a boy."[1]
    Ingrid Newkirk
    President, People for the Ethical Treatment of Animals

"How much more valuable is a man than a sheep!"
    Matthew 12:12 (NIV)

One of the most intriguing movies of the 1970's was *Planet of the Apes*. The movie was extremely popular and spawned several sequels and even a Saturday morning cartoon for kids. The premise of the movie was that astronauts had somehow been transported to the earth of the future. Men had nearly destroyed the entire planet. In the years that followed, apes became the dominant creatures on earth. Indeed, they had enslaved humans and also did experiments on them. Of course the astronauts were shocked at this turn of events and tried to help the humans.

Planet of the Apes was remade in 2001 with spectacular special effects. In fact, the quality of the special effects made this version even more disturbing than the original. Instead of looking like people in costumes as in the first movie, these "apes" seemed amazingly realistic in both appearance and behavior. Several scenes were quite unnerving. In one, a small ape in a dress picks out a little girl to take home in a cage to be her "pet." In another, apes are hunting and capturing humans. These scenes are difficult to watch because we are not used to seeing intelligent animals mistreating humans. As bad as it is to watch a human mistreat another human, it is worse to think about *animals* doing it.

Whether intentional or not, I believe that such movies have the effect of promoting an evolution worldview. From an evolutionary standpoint, all organisms are genetically related to every other organism. Therefore, there really is not much difference between men and animals. In the movie, the apes were upgraded and the humans downgraded, so the differences were blurred. In the same way, as evolution is promoted, the uniquely human characteristics are downplayed. Over and over we hear how similar we are to chimpanzees. Indeed, the mantra is "chimpanzees are our closest relatives."

Several years ago, I realized the impact of movies like *Planet of the Apes*. I started doing research on the differences between upright and quadrupedal walking. I watched a few video clips of a gorilla knuckle walking on all fours and it looked very strange. This puzzled me for quite some time until I realized why it seemed so unusual. I was so used to watching people in gorilla costumes that the real gorilla looked weird.

The human mind has an incredible capacity to fill in gaps and see relationships between things. So as one looks across the animal kingdom, there are obvious anatomical and behavioral similarities between man and the apes—more so than with any other creature. The question is: What does that similarity mean? Evolutionists insist that the similarity means common ancestry whereas the creationist focuses on the differences and views them as separately created. Whether the similarities or differences are emphasized will help to shape the conclusion regarding the presumed relationship between man and the apes.

There are several levels at which to compare and contrast apes and man. At the most basic level, the DNA and genetic similarity between chimpanzees and humans can be compared. Beyond that is comparative anatomy. Behavioral similarities such as language also must be taken into account. In addition to these types of similarities, fossil hominids have been used to suggest an evolutionary progression between man and apes.

176

Are Humans 98% Chimpanzee?[2]

For many years, evolutionary scientists—and science museums and zoos—have hailed the chimpanzee as "our closest living relative" and have pointed to the similarity in DNA sequences between the two as evidence. In most previous studies, they have announced 98-99% identical DNA.[3] However, these were for gene coding regions (such as the sequence of the cytochrome c protein), which constituted only a very tiny fraction of the roughly 3 billion DNA base pairs that comprise our genetic blueprint. Although the full human genome sequence has been available since 2001, the whole chimpanzee genome has not. Thus, all of the previous work has been based on only a fraction of the total DNA.

In the fall of 2005, in a special issue of *Nature* devoted to chimpanzees, researchers reported the draft sequence of the chimpanzee genome.[4] No doubt, this is a stunning achievement for science: deciphering the entire genetic make up of the chimpanzee in just a few years. Researchers called it "the most dramatic confirmation yet" of Darwin's theory that man shared a common ancestor with the apes. One headline read: "Charles Darwin was right and chimp gene map proves it."[5]

So what is this great and overwhelming "proof" of chimp-human common ancestry? Researchers have claimed that there is little genetic difference between us (only 4%). This is a very strange kind of proof because it is actually *double* the percentage difference that evolutionists have claimed for years![6] The reality is, no matter what the percentage difference, whether 2%, 4%, or 10%, they still would have claimed that Darwin was right.

Further, the use of percentages obscures the magnitude of the differences. For example, 1.23% of the differences are single base pair substitutions (1.06% are believed to be fixed differences.)[7] This doesn't sound like much until you realize that it represents about ~35 million mutations! But that is only the beginning, because there are ~40-45 million bases present in humans and missing from chimps, as well as about the same number present in chimps that is absent from man. These extra DNA nucleotides are called "insertions" or "deletions" because they are thought to have been added in or lost from the sequence. (Substitutions and

177

insertions are compared in the figure below.) This puts the total number of DNA differences at about 125 million. However, since the insertions can be more than one nucleotide long, there are about 40 million separate mutation events that would separate the two species.

To put this number into perspective, a typical 8½ x 11 page of text might have 4,000 letters and spaces. It would take 10,000 such full pages of text to equal 40 million letters! So the differences between humans and chimpanzees include ~35 million DNA bases that are different, ~45 million in the human that are absent from the chimp *and* ~45 million in the chimp that are absent from the human.

A G T C G T A C C   A G T C **G** T A C C

| | | | | | | | | | | | | | | |

A G T C **A** T A C C   A G T C   T A C C

Substitution   Insertion/deletion

Comparison between a base substitution and an insertion/deletion. Two DNA sequences can be compared. If there is a difference in the nucleotides (an A instead of a G) this is a substitution. In contrast, if there is a nucleotide base which is missing it is considered an insertion/deletion. It is assumed that a nucleotide has been inserted into one of the sequences or one has been deleted from the other. It is often too difficult to determine whether the difference is a result of an insertion or a deletion and thus it is called an "indel". Indels can be of virtually any length.

Creationists believe that God made Adam directly from the dust of the earth just as the Bible says. Therefore, man and the apes have never had an ancestor in common. However, assuming they did for the sake of analyzing the argument, then 40 million separate mutation events would have had to take place and become fixed in the population in only ~300,000 generations. This is an average of 133 mutations locked into the genome every generation. Locking in such a staggering number of mutations in a relatively small number of generations is a problem referred to as **"Haldane's dilemma."**[8] This problem is exacerbated because

178

most of the differences between the two organisms are likely due to neutral or random genetic drift. That refers to change in which natural selection is not operating. Without a selective advantage, it is difficult to explain how this huge number of mutations could become fixed in both populations. Instead, many of these may actually be intrinsic sequence differences from the beginning of creation.

There are many other differences between chimpanzee and human genomes that are not quantifiable as percentages.[9] Specific examples of these differences include:

1. Humans normally have 23 pairs of chromosomes while chimpanzees have 24. Evolutionary scientists believe that one of the human chromosomes has been formed through the fusion of two small chromosomes in the chimp instead of an intrinsic difference resulting from a separate creation. While this accounts for the difference in chromosome number, a clear mechanism for how a chromosomal abnormality becomes universal in a population.

2. At the end of each chromosome is a string of repeating DNA sequences called telomeres. Chimpanzees and other apes have about 23 kilobases (a kilobase is 1,000 base pairs of DNA) of repeats. Humans are unique among primates with much shorter telomeres only 10 kilobases long.[10]

3. While 18 pairs of chromosomes are 'virtually identical,' chromosomes 4, 9 and 12 show evidence of being 'remodeled.'[11] In other words, the genes and markers on these chromosomes are not in the same order in the human and chimpanzee. Instead of being 'remodeled' as the evolutionist suggest, these could, logically, also be intrinsic differences because of a separate creation.

4. Even with genetic similarity there can be differences in protein expression. Just because DNA sequences are similar does not mean that the same amounts of the proteins are produced. Such differences in protein expression can yield vastly different cellular responses.

179

Roughly 10% of genes examined showed significant differences in expression levels between chimpanzees and humans.[12]

5. Gene families are groups of genes that have similar sequences and also similar functions. Scientists comparing the number of genes in families have revealed significant differences between humans and chimpanzees. Humans have 689 genes that chimps lack and chimps have 86 genes that humans lack. Such differences mean that 6% of the gene complement is different between humans and chimpanzees irrespective of the individual DNA base pairs.[13]

Thus, the percentage of matching DNA is only one measure of how similar two organisms are and not really a good one at that. There are other factors besides DNA sequence that determine an organism's phenotype or the traits that are expressed. Indeed, even though identical twins have the same DNA sequence, as they grow older, twins show differences in gene expression.[14] Therefore, there must be some interaction between the genes and the environment.

Importantly, not all of the data supports chimp human common ancestry as nicely as evolutionists typically suggest. In particular, when scientists made a careful comparison between human, chimpanzee and gorilla genomes, they found a significant number of genetic loci where humans matched gorillas more closely than chimpanzees. Indeed, at 18-29% of the genetic loci, either humans and gorillas or chimpanzees and gorillas had a closer match to each other than chimpanzees and humans.[15] The authors of this study made the suggestion that perhaps chimpanzees and humans split off from a common ancestor, but later descendants of each reproduced to form chimp-human hybrids. Such an "explanation" appears to be an attempt to rescue the concept of chimp-human common ancestry rather than providing the data to confirm this hypothesis.

The similarity between human and chimpanzee DNA is really in the eye of the beholder. If you look for similarities, you can find them. But if you look for differences you can find those as well.

"Plagiarized Mistakes"

When a teacher has two tests submitted that are the same, it suggests that the two students cheated. However, if the students both got 100%, the fact that they are the same does not mean that they cheated. However, if the students both got 60% and had identical *incorrect* responses, then this would be convincing evidence that the students did in fact cheat. The teacher would believe that the students cheated because it is the best explanation for two students to have so many of the same mistakes. Plagiarized mistakes lead one to believe that they are both derived from a common source.

In the same way, evolutionists argue that there are plagiarized mistakes that are common in different types of organisms. They suggest that the *only* explanation for these similarities is that they are derived from the same common ancestor who had that mistake originally. They recognize that even though the DNA sequence of genes may be similar it is not necessarily proof of common ancestry. However, if there are "mistakes" or mutations that are the same, then this is much stronger evidence for common ancestry. Plagiarized mistakes in DNA sequences have been cited as powerful evidence in support of common descent.

There are two major categories of alleged "plagiarized mistakes." These are pseudogenes and endogenous retroviruses (ERVs). They are examples of the so called 'junk DNA.' Pseudogenes are stretches of DNA that have some of the characteristics of genes but are typically not expressed by cells. In some cases, such as olfactory receptors (smell detectors) humans have a large number of genes that appear to have been mutated so much that they are no longer functional. So this type of pseudogene is one that has lost its functionality. ERVs are stretches of DNA that can be spliced or copied and inserted into other locations within the genome. There are many different types of such mobile genetic elements.

The vitamin C pseudogene in particular has received considerable attention for its supposed support linking humans to the other primates. Most animals can make the vitamin C that they need whereas others must obtain it from their diet. There are several enzymes in the metabolic pathway that are required for cells to make this vitamin. In man and apes, they produce all but one of the enzymes in the pathway. They do not produce the enzyme gluconolactone oxidase (GLO) but they do have remnants of this gene. It is now a pseudogene and has been mutated so much that it is impossible for a functional protein to be produced.

Evolutionists have promoted this as a plagiarized mistake. Since apes and man both have the same gene that is messed up, they conclude that it must have been lost in a common ancestor. At first glance it would appear that indeed such evidence points to common ancestry. However, upon closer examination, it may appear differently.

An aspect of evolution that creationists can agree with is the fact that genes that are not selected for in a population are at great risk for mutation and loss. In the case of vitamin C, organisms that can obtain what they need from their diet do not need to make it themselves. In other words, if you get vitamin C from your diet, there is no selective advantage or pressure to maintain the gene and therefore we might expect it to be lost. So, God endowed all of these organisms with GLO to make vitamin C from the beginning. However, with the generations since the creation and Fall of man, the continued mutation of the gene left it damaged. There was no negative impact to the loss, because those organisms that lacked it could get what they needed from the food that they ate.

Many different organisms actually have lost the ability to produce vitamin C. While humans and apes stand out, there are others including guinea pigs, bats, and even certain fish. All have the same gene that has been mutated and is now dysfunctional. Therefore, just because two organisms have the same gene knocked out, it does not follow that they must have a common ancestor. Particularly with guinea pigs and bats, they would normally obtain sufficient vitamin C from their diets. This is also true of man and the apes. Thus, without selective pressure to maintain the gene for GLO, we should expect it to be lost, unable to be used again. Therefore, the fact that humans and chimpanzees have lost exactly the same gene is not all that convincing when it comes to common ancestry.

In a similar way, the ERVs and repeating DNA elements on the surface might seem to support common ancestry at first glance. However, in order to have a "plagiarized mistake" two conditions must be met. Both sources must be the same and there must be an error (or in this case a mutation without a function.) While there are examples of these mistakes in common, there are plenty of ones that are not.

After sequencing the chimpanzee genome, numerous differences in "junk DNA" were revealed.[4] Humans have many more short interspersed elements (SINEs) than chimps, but chimps have two novel families of retroviral elements which are absent from man. Comparing endogenous 'retroviral elements' yielded 73 human-specific insertions and 45 chimpanzee specific insertions. Humans have two SINE (Alu) families that the chimpanzees lack and humans have significantly more copies (~7,000 human specific copies vs. ~2,300 chimpanzee specific ones). There are also ~2,000 lineage specific L1 elements. All of these lineage specific changes would be required to take place sometime between the last chimp/human common ancestor, and the most recent common ancestor for all people on the planet. Importantly, these are modification for which there is no known selective advantage.

The ERVs do not always occur consistent with evolutionary expectations. For example, scientists analyzed the complement component $C4$ genes in a variety of primates.[16] Both chimpanzee and gorillas had short $C4$ genes. The human gene was long because of an ERV. Interestingly, orangutans and green monkeys had the same ERV inserted at exactly the same point. This is especially significant because humans are supposed to have a more recent common ancestor with both chimpanzees and gorillas and only more distantly with orangutans. Yet the same ERV in exactly the same position would imply that humans and orangutans had the more recent common ancestor. Here is a good case where ERVs do not line up with the expected evolutionary progression, nonetheless they are still held up as evidence for common ancestry.

Additional evidence has suggested that ERVs may in fact have functions.[17] An intriguing possibility is that one function of ERVs may have been to protect cells from infection by other viruses.

183

Key Skeletal Differences in Chimpanzees and Man

Besides the genetic differences between humans and chimpanzees, there are numerous skeletal differences. In fact, essentially every bone in the chimp is distinct from its counterpart in man. Many of the differences have to do with the means of locomotion. Since chimpanzees are knuckle walkers, their limb and finger proportions are different. A chimpanzee's arms are longer than their legs and their fingers are very long and curved. The long arms and long fingers help them endure the pressure from placing so much of their weight on their knuckles. The chimpanzee rib cage is barrel shaped and the spine is gently curved as a C. In humans, the rib cage is flatter and the spine is actually shaped more like an S. The S shape is important for upright walking. The chimpanzee legs go straight down whereas in humans our legs are angled inward so that our knees are closer together than the top of the legs. This allows humans to easily stand on one foot by shifting their weight. In contrast, chimpanzees have great difficulty walking on two legs.

The skulls of chimpanzees and humans are also vastly different. The braincase of man is usually more than double that of the chimpanzee. Chimps have very long and robust jaws with large canine teeth. The zygomatic arch (cheek bone) is much bigger to accommodate the larger jaw muscle. The face of

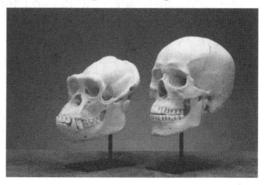

Comparison of the skulls of a chimpanzee (left) and human (right).

a chimpanzee is steep and sloped, whereas that of a human is flat and more vertical. Chimpanzees do not have a nasal bone but they do have a rather prominent brow ridge above the eyes.

An important distinction between the two skulls is in the location of the foramen magnum. The foramen magnum is the

184

hole in the base of skull where nerves pass between the brain and spinal cord. This hole is centrally located underneath the human skull. However, for apes, this hole is toward the back and indeed closer to a 45° angle. From the rear of the skulls, you can see the hole in all of the apes, but not in a human skull. The rear angled location of the foramen magnum allows these apes to hold their head with their eyes forward while walking on all fours. When humans try to go on all fours, the head must be tipped way back otherwise they would be looking straight at the ground.

Rear view of primate skulls. Skulls are (left to right) orangutan, male gorilla, female gorilla, chimpanzee, and human. For the apes, arrow indicates the location of the foramen magnum. Ape skulls are resting on a base that is the same color as the skull.

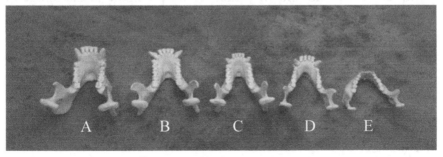

Primate jaw bones. Left to right: A) orangutan, B) male gorilla, C) female gorilla, D) chimpanzee, and E) human

Looking at the jaws of the primates reveals just how different the human jaw is compared to the apes'. Indeed, the human jaw is clearly the odd one out compared to the orangutan, gorilla, and

185

chimpanzee. The jaw muscles of the apes are significantly larger than mans' and thus they have a very powerful bite. Stedman and colleagues suggested that a mutation that reduced the size of human jaw muscles could have led to man's increased cranial capacity.[18] Since cranial capacity is determined by a variety of factors besides the jaw muscles, this hypothesis is quite unlikely.[19]

Anatomically, apes are much more similar to humans than any other animal. Although this has been interpreted by evolutionists as evidence for common ancestry, it can also be interpreted as common design. We live in the same world, breath the same air, eat some of the same food, we should expect some similarities. Regardless, we must be most similar to something! Even so, there are also significant anatomical differences between man and the apes. These should not be glossed over. When we look for similarities, we can find similarities, but when we look for differences, we can find the differences.

It is the differences that make the difference.

Conclusion

The fundamental question in the origins controversy comes down to the significance of man. Is the Bible correct, and man has been uniquely created in the image of God? Or is he warmed over pond scum after millions of years? If we are made in the image of God then this represents an intrinsic value that cannot be taken away. But if we are the product of millions of years of death, disease, bloodshed and survival of the fittest, then we are not worth much and have no intrinsic value.

When evolutionists insist that we have common ancestors with chimpanzees, rats, frogs and fish, it greatly devalues humanity. Indeed, the claim of Ingrid Newkirk, "A rat is a pig is a dog is a boy," expresses an evolutionary view in a nutshell. If evolution is correct, then why do we make distinctions between man and the beasts? From an evolutionary standpoint there really is no difference. Humans just got lucky in the random mutations department. If we are descended from apes, than we are living on a planet of apes.

186

Several years ago, I taught a section of research ethics at a state university. One of the important points I tried to emphasize was why humans have a different value than animals. I argued from the Declaration of Independence that a crucial assumption of democracy is that all people are "created equal." In the class was a student who was pursuing a Ph.D. in evolutionary biology. In her final paper, she chose the topic of human value to write about. She argued that she would like to say that humans have more value than animals, but could find no logical justification for it. Indeed, in an evolutionary sense, the only difference between a man and a monkey are the mutations that each accumulated over hundreds of thousands of generations.

The most important distinctive of man is this: When Jesus Christ the Son of the Living God came to earth...He did not come as a bacteria, an ameba, a dog or a monkey. He came as a man. "For God so loved the world that he sent his only begotten Son, that whosoever believes in him shall not perish but have eternal life." John 3:16 (NIV) God made people to reveal his glory in a unique way. It is only humanity that has this priceless gift of salvation by grace through faith. It is only the sons and daughters of Adam that can inherit so great a promise as to be called "children of the Lord."

---

[1] Vogue, September, 1989 and widely quoted since.

[2] Taken from DeWitt, David 2005. "Chimp Genome Sequence very Different from Man" *Jounral of Creation* **19**(3):5.

[3] Wildman, D.E., Uddin, M., Liu, G., Grossman, L.I. and Goodman, M. 2003, Implications of natural selection in shaping 99.4% nonsynonymous DNA identity between humans and chimpanzees: Enlarging genus *Homo, Proc. Natl. Acad. Sci. USA* **100**(12):7181-7188.

[4] The Chimpanzee Sequencing and Analysis Consortium 2005. "Initial sequence of the chimpanzee genome and comparison with the human genome." *Nature* **437**:69-87

[5] www.news-medical.net/?id=12840 31 Aug. 2005

[6] Studies of chimp-human similarity have typically ignored insertions and deletions although this accounts for most of the differences. A study by Roy Britten included these insertions and deletions and obtained a figure that is close to the 4% reported for the full sequence. See: Britten R.J., "Divergence between samples of chimpanzee and human DNA sequence is 5% counting indels" *Proceedings National Academy Science* **99**:13633-13635.

[7] Individuals within a population are variable and some chimps will have more or less nucleotide differences to man. This variation accounts for a portion of the differences. Fixed differences represent those that are universal. In other words, all chimpanzees have one nucleotide and all humans have a different one at the same position.

[8] ReMine, W.J. 2005. "Cost Theory and the cost of substitution—a clarification" *Journal of Creation* 19(1):113-125.

[9] Discussed in DeWitt, D.A. 2003. >98% Chimp/human DNA similarity? Not any more. *J. Creation* 17:8-10.

[10] Kakuo, S., Asaoka, K. and Ide, T. 1999. Human is a unique species among primates in terms of telomere length, *Biochem. Biophys. Res. Commun.* 263:308-314.

[11] Gibbons, A., 1998. Which of our genes make us human? *Science* 281:1432-1434.

[12] , Y., Oshlack, A., Smyth, G.K., Speed, T.P., and White, K.P. 2006. Expression profiling in primates reveals a rapid evolution of human transcription factors. *Nature* 440: 242-245.

[13] Demuth, J.P., De Bie, T., Stajich, J.E., Cristianini, N., and Hahn, M.W. The evolution of mammalian gene families PLoS ONE 1(1): e85. doi:10.1371/journal.pone.0000085

[14] Fraga, M.F., Ballestar, E., Paz, M.F., Ropero, S., Setien, F., Ballestar, M.L., Heine-Suner, D., Cigudosa, J.C., Urioste, M., Benitez, J., Boix-Chornet, M., Sanchez-Auilera, A., Ling, C., Carlsson, E., Poulsen, P., Vaag, A., Stephan, Z., Spector, T.D., Wu, Y-Z., Plass, C., Esteller, M. 2005. Epigenetic differences arise during the lifetime of monozygotic twins. Proc. Natl. Acad. Sci. USA 102(30): 10604-10609.

[15] Patterson, N., Richter, D.J., Gnerre, S., Lander, E.S. and Reich, D, 2006. Genetic evidence for complex speciation of humans and chimpanzees, *Nature* 441:315–321.

[16] Dangel, A.W., Baker, B.J., Mendoza, A.R. and Yu, C.Y. 1995. Complement component C4 gene intron 9 has a phylogenetic marker for primates: long terminal repeats of the endogenous retrovirus ERV-K(C4) are a molecular clock of evolution. *Immunogenetics* 42(1): 41-52

[17] Purdom, G. 2006. Human endogenous retroviruses (HERVs)—evolutionary "junk" or God's tools? http://www.answersingenesis.org/docs2006/1219herv.asp downloaded May 8, 2007.

[18] Stedman, H.H., Kozyak, B.W., Nelson, A., Thesier, D.M., Su, L.T., Low, D.W., Bridges, C.R., Shrager, J.B., Minugh-Purvis, N., and Mitchell, M.A. 2004. Myosin gene mutation correlates with anatomical changes in the human lineage, *Nature* 428: 415-418.

[19] DeWitt, D.A. 2005. Did a jaw muscle mutation lead to increased cranial capacity in man? *Journal of Creation* (formerly *TJ*) 19: 88-96.

10

Not by Chance

"The fit [between DNA and DNA binding proteins] is so good that it has been suggested that the dimensions of the basic structural units of nucleic acids and proteins evolved together to permit these molecules to interlock."

Molecular Biology of the Cell[1]

"I praise you because I am fearfully and wonderfully made; your works are wonderful, I know that full well."

Psalm 139:14 (NIV)

The Old Argument from Design

One of the most commonly used arguments for the existence of God is the argument from design—the recognition of the complexity and purpose observed in creation implies a Creator. The great Christian apologist William Paley wrote extensively on this point in his famous 1802 book *Natural Theology; or Evidences of the Existence and Attributes of the Creator.* Paley argued for the existence of God based on what is observed in life, the earth and the universe just as Paul said in Romans 1:20. Paley's approach was based on **teleology** which is the study of design or purpose in nature.

Paley's classic example was finding a watch. If you found a watch, you would know that it didn't always exist—there was a watchmaker who made it. It was produced for a purpose (keeping time). It has complex parts (spring etc.) and it has many integrative components that all work together to help it to carry out

189

its purpose. Therefore, when we consider living things which also have purpose and complexity, this implies that there is a designer

William Paley
1743-1805

who made living things. Paley wrote: "Wherever we see the marks of contrivance, we are led for its cause to an intelligent author. And this transition of the understanding is founded upon uniform experience."[2] Paley believed that intelligent causes could be inferred because the products would have an ultimate purpose, and interrelatedness of complex parts that cooperated to fulfill the purpose. Paley's book was very well received and was used for decades. In fact, Darwin had to read Paley's book while studying at Cambridge in 1831.

Philosopher David Hume allegedly refuted Paley's argument from design. Indeed, evolutionists often refer to Hume's "thorough critique"[3] of the argument from design. Hume may have pointed out weaknesses in Paley's argument, but it was not really an outright refutation. Hume's point was that the design argument is a weak analogy. We know about watches and we know that they have watchmakers. However, we don't really know what something designed by God should look like. In this case we must assume that living things are what God would make. Maybe it was made by some other god or space aliens. Further, since there are bad things in the world such as diseases, viruses, and cancer, it might imply that the designer was evil or incompetent.

A significant outcome of Darwin's theory of evolution was the ability for evolutionists to explain apparent design without a designer. Living things appear to have purpose and are very well suited to their environment. Paley thought that this was because of the way that God had made them. But Darwin proposed a new idea. The design was not real, but only *apparent*. Rather than being the result of purposeful design, they were the product of natural selection. Since natural selection would favor individuals in a population that were better suited to the environment, the

190

outcome would be organisms that were well adapted, but only *looked* like they were designed to be that way. Thus, evolutionists consider the design features to be illusory. This is why Francis Crick wrote: "Biologists must constantly keep in mind that what they see is not designed, but rather evolved."[4] Richard Dawkins elaborated on reasons why organisms that have evolved can give the appearance of design in his book *The Blind Watchmaker*.

Admittedly, Paley took his argument from design a bit too far. One cannot look at any living thing and from that alone conclude that the God of the Bible made it. The problem is that Paley combined general and special revelation. **General revelation** refers to the universal message from God that is evident in creation. What can be known about God through creation is very limited. It only reveals "God's invisible qualities—his eternal power and divine nature." (Romans 1:20 NIV) Through nature and general revelation one can know a little *about* God, but no one can *know* God apart from his Word.

Special revelation refers to the disclosure of God's truth by supernatural means such as miracles or the Scriptures. It is not accessible through human reason but is revealed to man only by God himself. When Jesus asked Peter, "Who do you say that I am?" Peter responded "You are the Christ, the Son of the living God." Then Jesus said "Blessed are you, Simon son of Jonah, for this was not revealed to you by man, but by my Father in heaven." (Matthew 16:16-17 NIV) There was nothing about Jesus that a person could conclude that he was the Christ using only human reason.

Most of what we know about God cannot be observed in nature. If there were no Scriptures and no special revelation we would not know God's will nor could we ever know it. There would be no Ten Commandments, we would not know of the Gospel or the Flood or the Fall in the Garden of Eden. Looking at creation alone we could learn nothing of the age of the earth or the reason for death in the world. All of this is special revelation.

Evidence and proof are not the same things. We cannot *prove* that God exists and that he is the Creator of all things, but this does not mean that there is no evidence to support it. There is evidence, but we must go beyond the physical evidence in nature alone and

191

include the Bible as evidence too. Ultimately, it is by faith. This is why Hebrews 11:3 says "By faith we understand that the universe was formed at God's command so that what is seen was not made out of what was visible." (NIV) There is nothing in the universe or in nature that would help us to know that the universe "was not made out of what was visible," or that it was "formed at God's command." We believe this through faith because the Bible says it.

So the person who looks at the complexity of life and concludes that God made it is actually using special revelation to come to the conclusion. For the person of faith, the evidence for God from nature is overwhelming. But they are looking at creation with knowledge from the Bible. The Scriptures inform how the evidence in nature is interpreted so it is not by human reason alone. Paley used his knowledge of Scripture to help him see the purpose and the grandeur of life.

During the Enlightenment, special revelation and miracles were downplayed. **Deism**, the belief in a distant, uninvolved creator who made the world but then simply left it to run itself was on the rise. With the de-emphasis on Scripture, many sought arguments and evidences that did not depend on the Bible at all. While Paley himself still believed that miracles were possible, he appealed to human reason on the basis of nature for evidence of the existence of God. However, human reason and wisdom provide a poor foundation for faith. Paul wrote in 1 Corinthians 2:4-5 (NIV) "My message and my preaching were not with wise and persuasive words, but with a demonstration of the Spirit's power, so that your faith might not rest on men's wisdom, but on God's power."[5]

The knowledge of God that can be gained from nature and human reason is limited to recognizing God's "eternal power and divine nature" as Romans 1:20 states. That general revelation is so clear that all men are without excuse if they fail to recognize it. Those who refuse to accept it cannot fathom the evidence for creation. Paul continued in 1 Corinthians 2:14 (NIV) "The man without the Spirit does not accept the things that come from the Spirit of God, for they are foolishness to him, and he cannot understand them, because they are spiritually discerned."[6] Thus, it requires a mustard seed of faith to be able to discern the evidence for creation. We must have faith as a starting point since "…without faith it is impossible to please God, because anyone who comes to him must believe that he exists and that he rewards those who earnestly seek him." Hebrews 11:6 (NIV)

Of course, it is possible to go too far the other way too. The opposite extreme is a "**God of the gaps**." People can be lazy and just attribute everything that they cannot comprehend to "God did it" or "That's just the way God made it." God has given us a mind and reason and he expects us to use them. There are many features of the earth and even the universe with unique parameters that allow for scientific investigation. Indeed, the earth is situated in a precise location that provides the opportunity to explore and understand the stars and galaxies of the universe.[7] The diversity of life on earth also provides numerous model systems for biologists to understand the process and mechanisms of life. Science, rightly interpreted from within a Biblical framework, can help us see more of the glory and wisdom of God and help us to know how the world works.

The Intelligent Design Movement

In the 1990's the Intelligent Design (ID) movement started in earnest fueled by several important books. In 1991, Phillip Johnson, a law professor at the University of California at Berkeley published *Darwin on Trial*, a critique of the evidence that is typically used to support Darwinian evolution. This book became something of a touchstone for ID. Johnson met with scientists and philosophers of science who had growing doubts about Darwinism. The Discovery Institute, a Seattle based think tank became a focal point for several key leaders of ID. Later in that decade, Intelligent Design became a household term after publication of Michael Behe's widely popular book, *Darwin's Black Box: The Biochemical Challenge to Evolution.* In this book, Behe laid the groundwork for the key ID concept of irreducible complexity. The other important concept is complex specified information as described by Bill Dembski.

The premise of ID is simply that design in nature is detectable. We are used to distinguishing between purposeful, intelligent causes and random, natural ones. An important aspect of an intelligent act is the combination of complexity and specificity. If we place SCRABBLE letters on a board randomly, we might find that it spells a few words—mostly two or three-letter words. However if you looked at the board and found that it spelled MEETMEAFTERSCHOOLNEXTFRIDAY, you would know right away that someone had left a message for you. The reason is because so many letters would not appear in a specific order without intelligence or purpose. This is specified complexity.

It is not necessary to know who or what an intelligent agent is in order to recognize the product of such an agent. For example, many people are working as part of the SETI program (Search for Extra Terrestrial Intelligence). These individuals are analyzing radio signals from space in the hopes of identifying a signal from space aliens. They believe that they can distinguish a signal from an intelligent race from random static noise. Even though we have no clue how these aliens would communicate, a non-random, purposeful signal would demonstrate an alien intelligence. Another example is the World Trade Center disaster. After the first plane hit, many may have thought "What a terrible accident!" However, when the second plane hit the other tower only minutes later, this was no accident. There was intelligent (and evil) purpose behind it. Even though we had absolutely no idea who it was, we knew there was a plot. So the specified complexity can provide information and evidence for intelligent agency even if the agent is unknown.

ID theory begins in the same way that Paley's design argument did. Instead of anatomical examples such as the eye, ID focuses on molecular examples such as the bacterial flagellum and the blood clotting cascade. Where Paley went beyond the evidence to claim that the design was evidence for God, ID theorists have been careful to stop at the evidence. In other words, scientific evidence may lead to the conclusion that a biochemical system was intelligently designed, but it does not provide any information as to the nature of the designer. ID proponents correctly recognize that special revelation is required to identify the designer. Most but not all ID proponents consider themselves Christian and believe that

194

the intelligent designer is God. They recognize that this is based on faith and not evidence from nature.

ID is in the precarious position of being criticized by evolutionists who say the design is only apparent as well as creationists who insist that the intelligent designer is God. Technically, ID makes no claim regarding who the "intelligent designer" is or the age of the earth. ID proponents span the spectrum of those who believe the earth is billions of years old to those who believe it is 6,000 years old. Phil Johnson has worked hard to try to get old earth creationists and young earth creationists to set aside their debate to work together to defeat the materialistic and naturalistic philosophy that has taken over science. This has been called the "Big Tent" strategy and has largely been successful.

ID has a place as part of evangelism. If it gets people to be open to the possibility that God exists, then there is a starting point to work from. However, just because someone believes in ID does not mean that they have become a Christian. It is also important to understand the difference between a Creator and an Intelligent Designer. God, the Creator, is intimately involved with the activity and created the "stuff", the matter and everything in the universe. A Designer, on the other hand, develops the plans but is not there to carry out the building—someone else does it. Moreover, a Designer is much more detached than a Creator. Therefore, to call God an "Intelligent Designer" is really to detract from his activity and involvement. ID can be used to remove obstacles that prevent people from trusting the Bible but it should not be an end in itself.

The major criticisms of ID are much the same as the challenges that Hume posed to Paley. (Weak analogy and examples of bad or destructive design) While ID proponents point to examples of irreducible complexity and claim design, evolutionists point to examples of natural selection and claim evolution. Additionally, critics cite the AIDS virus and a host of other diseases or examples of natural evil. Since many of these would also be considered evidence of design, it implies that the Designer is either evil or incompetent. ID would benefit from the answer that is available from the Bible. Because of the fall of man and the results of the curse on the whole universe, creationists have a much better answer for the problem of evil.

Irreducible Complexity

At the time Paley wrote *Natural Theology*, there really was no alternative explanation to account for the evidence of design in nature. Darwin provided such an alternative in his theory of evolution by natural selection. Since then, Darwinism has become the dominant view in virtually all of science. The question remains, however, whether Darwinian evolution really is the best explanation for all of the data. While evolution won the day in the late 1800's, does it remain as potent after the major advances in biochemistry and molecular biology of the last fifty years?

The biochemical challenge to Darwin is the complex molecular machines that have been found in cells. While living things and their organs appear complicated, they are nothing compared to the incredible molecular assemblies that are the basis for life in cells. Although scientists in the 1800's knew something of the chemical composition of cells, they had no clue about the regulation and processing of how life works. To them, the cell was very simple and just a blob of protoplasm. With the technology that is available today, we can manipulate genes, purify, sequence and determine the structure of proteins and, using microscopic equipment, watch the cell do what it does. Although we have much to learn, the cell is no longer the unknown "black box" that it was at the time of Darwin. Over the last few decades complex molecular machines have been discovered that make human designed inventions look simplistic. They pose a challenge to Darwinian evolution.

These molecular systems do not lend themselves to an explanation of origins by "numerous, successive slight modifications"[8] that Darwin acknowledged were necessary for evolution. The reason they don't is that they have a property that Michael Behe called **irreducible complexity**.

"By *irreducibly complex* I mean a single system composed of several well-matched parts that contribute to the basic

196

function, wherein the removal of any one of the parts causes the system to effectively cease functioning. An irreducibly complex system cannot be produced directly (that is, by continuously improving the initial function, which continues to work by the same mechanism) by slight, successive modifications of a precursor system, because any precursor to an irreducibly complex system that is missing a part is by definition non-functional. An irreducibly complex biological system, if there is such a thing would be a powerful challenge to Darwinian evolution. Since natural selection can only choose systems that are already working, then if a biological system cannot be produced gradually it would have to arise as an integrated unit, in one feel swoop, for natural selection to have anything to act on."[9] (Emphasis in original)

As an illustration in *Darwin's Black Box*, Behe used a mousetrap which has several well matched parts: platform, catch, hammer, spring and holding bar. All of the parts must be present to have a functioning mousetrap—with any of those pieces missing, it cannot catch a mouse. (Fusing two pieces together is cheating.) We could modify the mousetrap and select for ones that were better, however, how could it be built in the first place? If a piece is missing, it can't catch a mouse so there would be no selective advantage whatsoever to an incomplete mousetrap. This of course poses a problem if the mousetrap is going to be produced through a process of selection.

Behe then illustrated several important biochemical examples of molecular systems that require multiple integrated parts to be present from the beginning for the system to function. The bacterial flagellum self assembles using about 40 different proteins. The flagellum is a whip-like tail that spins much like an outboard motor and propels the bacterium through liquid. The blood clotting cascade uses over a dozen different proteins, most of them enzymes that specifically cut the next protein in the chain in order to activate it. A blood clotting cascade only works if you have all of the proteins present. Behe gave many other examples in his book.

The challenge of irreducible complexity to Darwinism, cuts to the very foundation of the theory itself, namely that complex organs can arise through natural selection instead of design. In Chapter 5 of this book, I opened with this quote from Darwin:

> "To suppose that the eye, with all its inimitable contrivances for adjusting the focus to different distances, for admitting different amounts of light, and for the correction of spherical and chromatic aberration, could have been formed by natural selection seems, I freely confess, absurd in the highest possible degree. Yet reason tells me that if numerous gradations from a perfect and complex eye to one very imperfect and simple, each grade being useful to its possessor, can be shown to exist; if further, the eye does vary ever so slightly, and the variations be inherited, which is certainly the case; and if variation or modification in the organ be ever useful to an animal under changing conditions of life, then the difficulty of believing that a perfect and complex eye could be formed by natural selection, though insuperable by our imagination, can hardly be considered real."

Darwin suggested, and his followers have complied, that if a graded series of organisms, each with some sort of eye can be found then this would mean that the eyes could have been produced by natural selection. This turns out to be a very good trick.

The reason that Darwin's argument is a trick is because it really uses circular reasoning. Let's say that such a graded series of organisms with increasingly complex eyes can be found in nature. One can only conclude that the eye was produced by natural selection if you start by assuming that all of the organisms share common ancestors. In other words, you must assume that evolution is true. Now, the fact is that such a graded series of organisms is found in nature from a single-celled euglena on up to a human eye. Setting up such a series does not explain *how* the human eye came to be. All it shows is that there are different organisms with different types of eyes in the world. Nonetheless, modern followers of Darwin still claim that all of this is evidence for evolution.

Darwin suggested that natural selection could account for the development of the human eye if it proceeded from simpler and less perfect eyes through a series of "numerous successive slight modifications. Some organisms such as a planaria (left) have simple eyespots. A fish eye (center) is more complex, but not to the extent of the human eye.

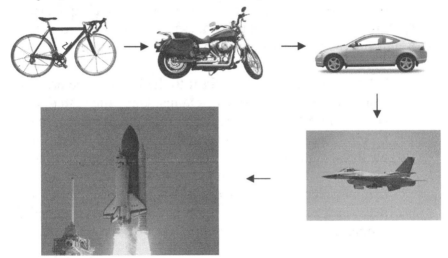

However, nearly anything can be put in an order such as bicycle, motorbike, car, jet, and space shuttle. Lining up objects or organisms does not explain *how* they came to be. It also does not demonstrate that natural selection is responsible for the change

Evolutionists often leave out the key ingredient necessary to account for an increase in complexity: information. For example, scientists had supposedly addressed a major criticism that creationists level against evolution—the absence of a genetic mechanism that would significantly alter the body plan of animals. The research of McGinnis and colleagues[10] seemed to suggest that a mutation in a particular Hox gene was sufficient to suppress the

199

development of legs. This mutation was believed to be responsible for the conversion of shrimp-like creatures with many legs into insect-like creatures with only 6 legs. However, this is really just a straw man argument because creationists do not claim that mutations cannot alter the body plan. Rather, they claim that mutations do not lead to an increase in information. Indeed, reducing the number of legs may alter the body plan but it does not explain the origin of legs in the first place. Nor does it explain where the genetic information to produce wings came from. Successful macro-evolution requires the addition of NEW information and NEW genes that produce NEW organs and systems.[11]

Ken Miller is arguably Michael Behe's principle antagonist and very much opposed to ID. In his own book, *Finding Darwin's God*, Miller argued strenuously against irreducible complexity quoting from the same passage from Darwin just above.

> "Darwin's reasoning cuts right to the heart of the argument from design. It boldly claims that the interlocking complexity of a multipart organ like the eye could indeed be produced by natural selection. How? As Darwin noted all that we really need to show is existence of 'numerous gradations' from the simple to the complex. Then all natural selection has to do is to favor each step in the pathway from simple to complex and we have solved the problem.
>
> "The crux of the design theory is the idea that by themselves, the individual parts or structures of a complex are useless. The evolutionist says no, that's not true. Those individual parts can indeed be useful, and it's by working on those 'imperfect and simple' structures that natural selection eventually produces complex organs."[12]

Although Miller makes it sound like evolution has everything worked out, in fact, it is just hand waving. Lining up a series of eyes does not demonstrate that natural selection "favors each step in the pathway." It begs the question because how many steps are

200

required *between* each type of eye? If we wanted to convert a bicycle into a space shuttle with intermediates such as a motorcycle, automobile, and airplane, we would need to do a lot more than line them up in a gradual sequence. Behe might argue that all Miller has is a series of separate irreducibly complex structures.

Miller has used this same line of reasoning to attack the irreducible complexity of the bacterial flagellum. He uses an argument called **co-option** in which evolution takes advantage of a system that was used for one thing and turns it into something else. In this way, natural selection is supposed to favor the evolution of a simple system that can then be modified or added to. Therefore, the entire system as it exists now does not need to be present from the start.

As a key intermediate in the evolution of the flagellum, Miller points to a structure called the Type Three Secretory System (TTSS).[13] Bacteria such as *Yersinia pestis* (the pathogen that causes bubonic plague) use this structure as a micro-syringe to inject toxins into cells. The TTSS does contain 8-10 proteins that have a great deal of similarity to some of the normal flagellar proteins. At first glance, this would seem to favor co-option since there is a simpler system that has a different function that could be selected for. However, with a more thorough analysis, it would appear that the TTSS may actually represent a *broken* flagellar system.[14] Rather than being an intermediate step on the way to evolving a flagellum, the TTSS could be the remnants of a flagellar system that is missing most of the other components. The degeneration and loss of ~30 proteins is a much more likely scenario than the production of 8-10 novel proteins through random mutation.

Conclusion

The argument from design makes a very powerful case for the existence of God. However, one must be willing to consider the evidence in order to appreciate it and recognize the Creator through what he has made. Even in spite of evidence, people often reject the truth of God. In Romans 1:18-23, Paul refers to those "who suppress the truth" and who "exchange the truth of God for a lie." The evidence from nature can provide sufficient rationale only for understanding the invisible qualities of God. To *know* God—who he is—requires faith and the study of the Bible.

My good friend and colleague Dr. Terry Spohn has coined the term bio-logian to describe creationist biologists. These are people who study living things and do so recognizing the God who made it. Instead of chalking up the wonderful design and integrative complexity to random chance and natural selection, it is so rewarding to give the praise to God and recognize his wisdom. As I have studied cell biology and conduct my research, I do a lot of work with a microscope. Through the microscope I can see intimate details of living cells. When I do, I am often reminded of the fact that the closer we look at things that man has made, the more we see the flaws. However, when you examine what God made, the closer you look at the *better* it seems.

---

[1] Alberts, B., Johnson, A., Lewis, J., Raff, M., Roberts, K., and Walter, P. 2002. *Molecular Biology of the Cell* 4th Ed. Garland Science pp. 384. Bruce Alberts has served as president of the National Academy of Science and is an evolutionist.

[2] Paley, W. 1802. *Natural Theology*

[3] Sonleitner, F. J., 2004. What's wrong with Pandas?—A word to the teacher. National Center for Science Education November 24, 2004 http://www.ncseweb.org/resources/articles/2127_58_sonleitner_what39s_wr_11_24_2004.asp

[4] Crick, Francis 1988. *What Mad Pursuit* (New York: Basic Books), 138

[5] The entire passage from 1 Corinthians 1:18-2:16 gives an excellent explanation of the role of human reason and wisdom compared with the work of the Holy Spirit.

[6] My colleague Steve Deckard drew my attention to this passage in relation to creation.

[7] Gonzales, G. and Richards, J. *Privileged Planet*

[8] Darwin, Charles 1859. On the Origin of Species.

[9] Behe, Michael J. 1996. *Darwin's Black Box* Free Press

[10] Ronshaugen, M., McGinnis, N., and McGinnis, W. 2002. Hox protein mutation and macroevolution of the insect body plan. *Nature*: **415**(6874) 914-917.

[11] DeWitt, David A. 2002. Hox Hype: Has macro-evolution been proven? http://www.answersingenesis.org/docs2002/0215hox_hype.asp downloaded April 30, 2007.

[12] Miller, Ken R. 1999. *Finding Darwin's God* Harper Collins p135-136.

[13] Miller, KR. 2004. The Bacterial flagellum unspun. In W. A. Dembski & M. Ruse (Eds.), *Debating Design: From Darwin to DNA,* pp.81-97. Cambridge: Cambridge University Press.

[14] Minnich, S.A. and Meyer, S.C. Genetic analysis of coordinate flagellar and type III regulatory circuits in pathogenic bacteria
http://www.discovery.org/scripts/viewDB/filesDB-download.php?id=389

11

Life from Life

"It is often said that all the conditions for the first production of a living organism are present, which could ever have been present. But if (and Oh! what a big if!) we could conceive in some warm little pond, with all sorts of ammonia and phosphoric salts, light, heat, electricity, etc., present, that a protein compound was chemically formed ready to undergo still more complex changes...."

Charles Darwin[1]

"And God said, "Let the water teem with living creatures, and let birds fly above the earth across the expanse of the sky." So God created the great creatures of the sea and every living and moving thing with which the water teems, according to their kinds, and every winged bird according to its kind. And God saw that it was good."

Genesis 1:20-21 (NIV)

One of the most perplexing questions in all of biology is how life arose on the planet. Up until a few hundred years ago, most people believed in **spontaneous generation**. This is the idea that living things can arise from non-living material. Indeed, they had observed maggots and worms "appear" in dead animals or meat that was left to spoil. Unaware of the microscopic eggs, the spontaneous generation of living things seemed like a reasonable conclusion.

In 1668, an Italian physician named Francisco Redi tested the idea of spontaneous generation. By covering meat in a jar, he prevented the formation of maggots. This suggested that the maggots came only when flies could access the meat. Redi suggested that the "Creator has never since produced any kinds of plants or animals…and everything which we know in past or present times that … has produced came solely from the true seeds of the plants and animals themselves, which thus…preserve their species." Thus, Redi believed that God had ceased his creative activity after the creation week and all "new" creatures came from the seeds of creatures that were made at the beginning.

While people understood that large creatures such as flies and worms came from eggs, the origin of the tiny microscopic bacteria and other single celled creatures remained an enigma. In 1864, Louis Pasteur designed an ingenious experiment that settled the spontaneous generation debate. Heating broth in a flask with an S shaped neck; he showed that microbes could not arise from broth alone but only from other microbes. Pasteur made the firm statement: "All life from life." In other words, the only way to get living things is to have them come from other living things. Pasteur also said, "Never will the doctrine of spontaneous generation recover from the mortal blow of this simple experiment. No, there is now no circumstance known in which it can be affirmed that microscopic beings came into the world without germs, without parents similar to themselves."[2]

Louis Pasteur
(1822-1895)

Pasteur was right—almost. For about five decades, it was impossible to discuss the origin of life outside of a theological context. Since living things must come from *pre-existing* living things, this presents the obvious problem of where the first living thing came from. Even though many scientists had begun to accept Darwin's theory of evolution, the obstacle of the origin of life remained. Thus, while Darwin's theory might explain the origin of species, it held no hope for explaining the origin of life in the first place. In the early 1920's a Russian chemist named

206

Oparin began to speculate on how chemicals might have coalesced to become the first living cell.

Only three options are possible to explain the origin of life. The first is that living things were made by a Creator. However, this option upsets the naturalistic philosophy that dominates science and is typically excluded on principle. Another option is that life came to earth from outer space. Such a possibility is not subject to scientific investigation and really begs the question. If we want an answer to the origin of life question, saying that it arose in space first only pushes the answer aside. The last option is **abiogenesis**—the process of how life is supposed to arise through the coming together of molecules coupled with natural selection.

Many scientists have accepted the idea of abiogenesis which means "life from non-life". As will be discussed throughout this chapter, they believe that natural laws and processes can account for the origin of life without intervention from a Creator. They believe that molecular reactions coupled with natural selection was able to produce self replicating systems that subsequently gave rise to the first living cell. Although abiogenesis and spontaneous generation both have life coming from non-living starting material, in the case of abiogenesis, the process is believed to have taken millions of years. **Ironically, the only real distinction between abiogenesis and spontaneous generation then is that abiogenesis is not very *spontaneous* at all.**

Scientists believe that life arose on earth very soon after the earth had cooled. This is because they have found fossilized bacteria and **stromatolites** in strata which have been radiometirically dated to 3.5-3.8 billion years ago (using evolutionary dating systems.) Stromatolites are banded columns of limestone or chert. They form from mounded colonies of cyanobacteria (blue-green, photosynthetic algae) which trap fine sediment. When these fossils form, all that is left are the thin sedimentary layers with no remains of the organisms that were once present.

Although we have evidence of life on earth such as this, there is really no evidence in nature that indicates how or where that life came from. Thus, scientists are left to piece together a history of events as to how life arose by looking at living things. One approach has been reductionistic, teasing apart individual processes and steps and explaining how each could work in a naturalistic scenario. A problem with this approach is that conditions that might allow one process to occur may actually preclude another, so it does nothing to solve the problem of the origin of life. In order to address the question of whether a naturalistic explanation of the origin of life is plausible, it will be helpful to examine what life requires in the first place.

What is Life Anyway?

Living things share many important characteristics that distinguish them from non-living things. While scientists may disagree on what specifically constitutes a living thing, there are certain criteria that appear universal for life on earth:

Organized—Living things are organized whether a large multi-cellular organism or one that consists of a single cell. Large organisms are made up of many different coordinated parts. Even a bacterium can have distinct compartments within it.

Made of cells—All living things are made of one or more cells. Cells are the fundamental unit of life.

Obtain and use energy—A living thing must be supplied continuously with energy in order to maintain itself. This energy is used to carry out many of the chemical reactions that take place inside cells. Plants harness energy from the sun and use it to produce sugars. Animals derive their energy from eating plants or other animals that ate plants. Fungi and decomposers can obtain their energy through consuming dead organic material. Some organisms such as chemosynthetic bacteria obtain energy through specific chemical reactions.

Metabolism—Metabolism is used to obtain and use energy, but the process is also required to produce or dispose of all of the chemical components within cells. The chemical building blocks—including the nucleotides that make up DNA, the amino acids that make up proteins, and the fatty acids that make up lipids—all must be produced, maintained, and disposed of properly. Cells require numerous enzymes to carry out the reactions necessary to produce or degrade all of the chemical components in cells. Those that the cells or organisms cannot make themselves must be obtained from the environment from other organisms that can make them.

Response to the environment—All living things respond in certain ways to conditions in the environment. These can be cues for growth or danger. Organisms also seek to maintain homeostasis. Deviations are detected and the organism reacts to counterbalance the change.

Change or Growth—Living things undergo a maturation process of growth and change. Even single celled organisms grow following cell division.

Reproduction—All living things are produced by living things through a process of reproduction. Single celled organisms replicate by splitting into two. Multi-cellular organisms have specialized cells that are involved in reproduction. Viruses cannot independently reproduce themselves and thus are not alive.

In order to be considered "alive" all of the above characteristics must be present to a certain degree. (For example, an organism that is sterile for some reason is still considered alive.) These characteristics are common to everything from bacteria to man.

Minimal Requirements for Life

The characteristics of living things make for quite a list—a list that exposes a major obstacle, namely, where does life come from? In trying to construct a plausible scenario for the origin of life, it will be useful to consider the minimal elements that would be necessary for an initial stage. In other words, what is the bare minimum that would be required in order to have the characteristics of life? In moving from inanimate matter and chemicals to a living thing, the following must be involved:

1. Metabolism: the ability to obtain and use energy
2. Boundary: used to separate self from non-self
3. Hereditary material: to pass on information
4. Controlled reproduction: not just splitting but a regulated process to allow life to continue.

These features must be simultaneously present for life. All of these are required and interdependent on each other. Without any one of them, it would be impossible to have life. This section will discuss these key requirements for life and why they must all be present in the first living thing.

1. Metabolism

Living things need to carry out a variety of chemical reactions to repair and maintain themselves, to produce and use energy and to reproduce. This requires enzymes, proteins or other molecules of a specific sequence to carry out the reactions. In the absence of a boundary, these molecules would simply be free in solution. Thus, a boundary is necessary in order to carry out metabolism. Hereditary information is required in order to replace the metabolic enzymes as well as to reproduce them. Without controlled reproduction, daughter cells might end up with too much or insufficient amounts of the metabolic proteins. Living cells have hundreds of metabolic molecules that carry out the reactions that are needed. Therefore, a boundary, hereditary material and controlled reproduction are required for a cell to carry out metabolism.

2. Boundary

A boundary is necessary from the beginning in order to have a living thing. Without a boundary, all of the organic molecules will simply be free in the organic soup. The boundary is needed in

210

order to sequester and concentrate specific molecules. However, once a boundary is in place, this creates additional problems. First, certain desired molecules need to be able to cross the boundary and unwanted waste molecules need to be exported. Maintaining the boundary requires repair and replacement of the components and thus, metabolism. Hereditary instructions are necessary to provide the information needed for maintaining the boundary as well as producing the molecules involved in transport. If reproduction is not controlled, there could be insufficient molecules when the cell divided. Alternatively, reproduction might not occur at all. The cell membrane serves as the boundary for living cells. Thus, metabolism, hereditary material and controlled reproduction are all required for a living thing to have and maintain a boundary.

3. Hereditary information

Living things must have hereditary materials in order to pass instructions to each new offspring. Without such hereditary material, there are no instructions that provide the program for the organism. However, hereditary information must be sequestered and enclosed within a boundary; otherwise it is simply free in the organic soup. The hereditary material would need to be maintained, repaired, replaced and reproduced. This would require metabolic processes to maintain. Controlled reproduction would be necessary in order to ensure that each offspring received a complete set of instructions. Thus, metabolism, a boundary and controlled reproduction are all required for a living thing to properly make use of hereditary material.

4. Controlled reproduction

Living things need an elaborate control mechanism to regulate reproduction. Reproduction of a cell is not simply cutting the material in half. A controlled process ensures that each offspring receives all of the material that is needed. It also ensures that the boundary is not breeched during the process of division. The control of reproduction is an active process and therefore would require metabolism to carry out. Hereditary instructions are necessary to provide the reproduction control mechanism. The boundary allows for the propagation and production of new living things. Numerous proteins and enzymes are essential for the regulation of cell division in living things. Living things are much more than just a collection of molecules.

Miller and the "Building Blocks of Life"

Although Oparin had proposed a "primordial soup" of organic compounds on the early earth in the early 1920's it was roughly 30 years before anyone really tested the idea. While a graduate student with Harold Urey, Stanley Miller assembled an apparatus to simulate pre-biotic conditions of the early earth. He placed several starting materials inside the chamber including water, and the gases methane, ammonia, and hydrogen. He attached electrodes that would spark the chamber and simulate lightning. After a week, he analyzed the compounds that were present in the chamber and found that several amino acids, amino acid precursors and hydrogen cyanide (HCN) had been produced. HCN was important because this can be converted into adenine, the nitrogen base for ATP which is used as a nucleotide in DNA and as the energy currency in cells.

This experiment was celebrated as producing the "building blocks of life." Proteins are key components of living things and they are made up of amino acids. Thus, producing amino acids spontaneously without living things was viewed as a major breakthrough. The Miller experiment has been featured in nearly every biology textbook as providing important clues for the origin of life on earth. However, there is much more to this story.

First, to put the Miller experiment in context, we must consider the work of a German chemist named Fredrick Wohler. In the early days of organic chemistry, in the early 1800's, scientists believed that the chemistry of living things was special. They thought only living things could produce organic molecules. Wohler did the unthinkable. Upon heating ammonium cyanate, he discovered that it made urea. Urea is produced by living things and is a primary component of urine. However, Wohler had made this compound in a lab which was exactly like the compound made

212

by living things. This was a huge breakthrough and showed that living things obeyed the laws of chemistry and physics—that there was nothing really special about them chemically.

Wohler's observation can be extended to other aspects of living things. Because the molecules in living things obey the same laws of chemistry and physics that non-living do, it is no surprise that we can synthesize almost every compound made in living things. There is nothing unique about the amino acids that cells make, and we can make amino acids in a laboratory. If we have the right enzymes and other components, we can replicate DNA molecules; we can synthesize proteins and many other compounds. In this context, the results of Miller's experiment are really inevitable. Synthesizing amino acids or other chemicals in a laboratory demonstrate that the compounds are made by unguided natural processes. Technically speaking, there is nothing particularly remarkable about Miller's ability to make an apparatus that could produce amino acids.

While Miller was able to make about half of the 20 amino acids that are common in proteins, such origin of life scenarios do not produce all of them. Further, there are many other amine compounds that are made which are not found in proteins. Another complication is the fact that such synthetic reactions produce a mixture of what are called left and right handed amino acids. These amino acids are mirror images of each other, however, only left handed amino acids comprise the proteins in all living things on earth.

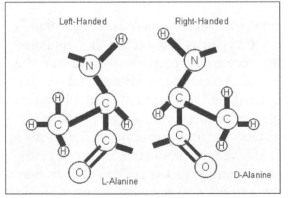

When amino acids are made in a laboratory, they are always produced in two forms—mirror images of each other. Only the left handed form is used to make proteins in living things.

213

Making amino acids is hardly producing the "building blocks of life." Even if amino acids are present, these must be assembled into proteins. For two amino acids to join together and form a peptide bond, energy input is required. Even if the amino acids can be joined together, they must do so in a specific sequence in order to make a functional protein. In living things, DNA provides the information for the assembly of amino acids into the right sequence for functional proteins. But even having proteins is not enough to have life. Claiming that amino acids are the building blocks of life is the equivalent of saying that nails are the building blocks of a skyscraper.

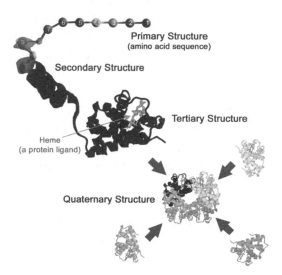

The sequence of amino acids in a protein determines how that protein will fold up and what three dimensional shape the protein will adopt. The function of a protein is determined by the structure. Changes in the amino acid sequence can impact the overall structure and thus alter the function of the protein.

In origin of life simulations like Miller's there is one gas that is always excluded: oxygen. Oxygen is left out of the simulated primitive earth atmosphere because oxygen would prevent the amino acids from forming at all. Scientists assumed that oxygen was not present on the early earth and only accumulated after there were photosynthetic bacteria to produce the oxygen. However, evidence is accumulating that the composition of the earth's atmosphere would not have allowed the production of amino acids. In particular, scientists are beginning to recognize that oxygen may have been present from the earliest stages of earth history.[3] In addition, UV light from the sun would be expected to destroy

214

methane and ammonia if they were present in the early earth atmosphere. This problem would be exacerbated without a protective ozone layer which could only be available if oxygen were present. Instead of methane, ammonia, and hydrogen gas, as has been used in the atmospheric simulations, geoscientists now suggest the atmosphere was mostly nitrogen, oxygen and carbon dioxide—conditions that would not permit the production of amino acids in sufficient quantity. Without the ability to form HCN, there is also no way to make nucleotide precursors which are necessary for producing DNA and RNA molecules.

Since the prospects for the production of amino acids in a primitive earth atmosphere seem bleak, scientists have posed two other sources for amino acids on a pre-biotic earth. Since meteorites have been shown to have traces of amino acids in similar ratios to those obtained from spark discharge experiments, they have been proposed as a potential source. This would require a billion years worth of meteor bombardment to provide the organic material necessary for life. A problem with this scenario is a lack of evidence for that much meteor and comet activity and difficulty extracting the organic compounds from the rocks. The other popular alternative is that the necessary reactions took place in thermal vents in the depths of the ocean.

Regardless of the source of amino acids, origin of life researchers must still account for the production of functional protein molecules and cells. Sydney Fox has suggested there were **protenoids** first. These would be polypeptides of random sequence that can form from heating dry amino acids. Such protenoids can form globular structures called microspheres. These microspheres can accumulate nucleic acids, lipids or other molecules. In this way, they can appear to grow. They can also split apart (like a bubble breaking into two smaller bubbles). Although this may look like cell growth and division it is neither. Cell growth and division is a very tightly controlled process even in the simplest bacterium and is nothing like the fission of molecular globules.

The "RNA World"

A major obstacle to the use of amino acids and proteins as the first chemical compounds in origin of life scenarios is the lack of a mechanism for sequence specificity. There is nothing in a protein to provide information to allow for replication of that protein. However, DNA and RNA both can serve as a template that will allow for replication. Because of the nucleotide base pairing (A with G and C with T or U) one molecule of nucleic acid contains the information to produce an exact replica of itself. Thus, nucleic acid has the capacity to serve as hereditary material—it can be copied and provided to each new daughter cell.

The use of DNA as the starting molecules in the origin of life has its own set of obstacles. First, the information content found in the order of nucleotides in DNA must come from somewhere. Second, even with such a mechanism, there is no way to convert the DNA code into protein without having proteins in the first place—a classic chicken or egg conundrum. Moreover, proteins are required for the replication of DNA which makes this molecule less useful as a starting point in the origin of life. That leaves RNA to play the starring role.

In living cells, the amino acid sequence of a protein is ultimately determined by the sequence of nucleotide bases in DNA. The DNA sequence is converted into a corresponding polymer of RNA nucleotides through a process called **transcription**. RNA molecules are then transported to protein factories called **ribosomes**. Once at the ribosome, the nucleotides are read three at a time, and converted into an amino acid sequence. This is called **translation**. During translation, three RNA nucleotides are matched to a specific molecule called a transfer RNA (tRNA). The tRNAs have a cloverleaf structure with RNA bases called **codons**.

What I have just described in a few sentences can seem like a simple, straightforward process. It is not. What we know about the details and regulation of protein production would fill an entire book and even then, only gloss over it. In addition, the mechanism of translating the nucleotide code into an amino acid sequence is a very complex process. Of the 64 possible codons, (combinations

216

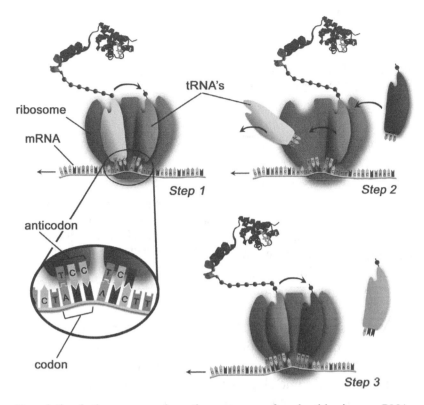

tRNA's

ribosome

mRNA

Step 1

Step 2

anticodon

codon

Step 3

Translation is the process where the sequence of nucleotides in an mRNA molecule is converted into a sequence of amino acids to make a protein. It takes place at a "protein factory" called a ribosome. The ribosome is a complex assembly of many different proteins and rRNA molecules. Ratcheting three bases at a time, the ribosome matches nucleotides from each codon in mRNA to a corresponding anticodon in a tRNA. Each tRNA is specific for a particular amino acid. The tRNA carries an amino acid which is linked to the growing protein chain. When a stop signal is reached, the whole assembly breaks apart and releases the new protein.

of 3 nucleotide bases) 61 of them are used to code for different amino acids. (Several different codons can be translated as the same amino acid.) Then there are the enzymes! Special enzymes called amino acyl tRNA synthetases attach a specific amino acid to the appropriate tRNA molecule that has the anticodon for that amino acid. Each of the 20 amino acids has its own enzyme that binds it to the correct tRNA. Thus, it is these enzymes that are ultimately responsible for the translation of the genetic code. Scientists understand a great deal about how this process works and yet are at a loss to explain *how* it came to be. These enzymes are required for the translation process *and yet the enzymes are themselves a product of the translation process!* The best they can say is that it was a "frozen accident" and once it happened, it could never happen again. Notice that this is not an explanation of *how* but an assumption that it happened.

Molecular model of a tRNA with an amino acid. Each tRNA has an end which binds to an amino acid and an end with an anti-codon.

The process of protein production with a DNA sequence code, RNA intermediates, ribosome protein factories and tRNA translation intermediates is common in every living thing on earth. Although there are some slight differences in the genetic code of a few organisms, different types of ribosomes, and obviously different DNA sequences, all life on earth has the same hereditary material and makes proteins in essentially the same way. Because this process is the same for all life, evolutionists view it as strong evidence for common ancestry. An equally plausible, although non-naturalistic explanation, is that it was designed by a common Creator.

Evolutionary scientists have held out hope for what is called an "**RNA world**." Because of the problems of sequence specificity and heredity intrinsic to proteins and the necessity of proteins for DNA utilization, RNA appears to be the best solution for the first molecules of life. RNA can serve as a hereditary material and indeed is the genetic instructions found in certain viruses like HIV. In addition, some RNA molecules have limited enzymatic ability and these are called **ribozymes**. Ribozymes have a limited range of reactions that can be catalyzed and are not as diverse in

218

functionality as protein enzymes can be. Most of the known functions for ribozymes involve cleavage and splicing of other RNA molecules. Still, the combination of hereditary capacity and enzymatic functionality gives scientists hope that the first living things were strictly RNA based.

First position	Second position				3rd	
U	U	C	A	G		
	Phe	Ser	Tyr	Cys	U	
	Phe	Ser	Tyr	Cys	C	
	Leu	Ser	Stop	Stop	A	
	Leu	Ser	Stop	Trp	G	
C	Leu	Pro	His	Arg	U	
	Leu	Pro	His	Arg	C	
	Leu	Pro	Gln	Arg	A	
	Leu	Pro	Gln	Arg	G	
A	Ile	Thr	Asn	Ser	U	
	Ile	Thr	Asn	Ser	C	
	Ile	Thr	Lys	Arg	A	
	Met (start)	Thr	Lys	Arg	G	
G	Val	Ala	Asp	Gly	U	
	Val	Ala	Asp	Gly	C	
	Val	Ala	*Glu*	Gly	A	
	Val	Ala	*Glu*	Gly	G	

The genetic code uses three consecutive nucleotides of messenger RNA to specify a particular amino acid. The chart indicates the standard code that is common to virtually all organisms on earth. There are some variant genetic codes but these tend to be rare. Notice that there is some redundancy in the code. For example, GAG and GAA both code for glutamic acid.

Even with all the promise that the idea of an RNA world holds there are serious problems. RNA is a poor option to use for hereditary material for two major reasons. First, it is extremely unstable and easily degraded. Second, because it is single stranded, there is no means of repair. The double stranded nature of DNA allows repairs to be made because there is a still a template even when one base is lost. In a single stranded template like RNA, once a base is lost, it is impossible to repair it. The problem of sequence specificity remains in an RNA world. The best solution here is that people think clays could have served as a starter template to make RNA molecules. While these have been shown to facilitate the formation of RNA, it remains to be seen how a functional RNA could form spontaneously from a clay template. Further, the sugar ribose which is found in RNA cannot be made in any appreciable amount in origin of life simulations. This has caused some scientists to speculate that there was some other precursor molecule that was used before RNA but they have absolutely no clue what that molecule could have been.

When it comes to the RNA world, speculation is rampant. However, even to get an RNA world requires imagination. What this really means is that there is no good explanation whatsoever for how inorganic molecules came together to form the first living cell. As scientists perform experiments and appear to solve one of the problems in the necessary chain of events it exposes another problem. Alternatively, the solution to one small piece of the puzzle is utterly incompatible with other pieces of the puzzle.

I have often wondered why so many scientists have spent so much time and money trying to discern a process for how life could arise simply by natural laws and processes. The time and money might be better spent trying to raise the dead. Instead of putting the molecules together in just the right arrangement to produce life, why not start with something that is dead? All of the pieces would be there almost in the right ratios and arrangements. It should be much easier to bring something back to life or keep it from dying in the first place. Yet scientists know that they can't do that and don't try. Life, in some way, is more than the chemicals. As Pasteur put it, "Life only comes from life."

At the end of the day, the real problem is a heart problem. They cannot accept a Creator, because if there is a Creator, then there is someone to whom they are accountable. So no matter how ridiculous or outlandish the origin of life scenario is, some individuals will hold to it in order to resist the obvious fact that life was created.

Little Green Men

Faced with the hurdles implicit in explaining the origin of life on earth through natural laws and processes, some scientists have given up. Increasing numbers of scientists are seriously considering the possibility that life on earth came from outer space. The problems with working out the chemistry on earth seem insurmountable, so the next best solution is to push the problem out into space. The idea that life on earth was seeded from space is called **panspermia**. Francis Crick, co-discoverer of the structure of DNA is one of the scientists that initially proposed this idea. While pushing the problems in chemistry aside, it raises other problems. Life would have to survive the journey of course, but then it has to travel millions and millions of miles to get here.

Although life coming from space is not something that can really be tested scientifically, nonetheless, it is often included as a possibility in biology textbooks. However, the possibility of creation or design is excluded. Since the origin of life is really a historical problem rather than an empirical one, experiments alone will not be able to prove any scenario. Therefore, all explanations should remain as possibilities and the one that covers the most observations with the fewest problems is the one that should be held. Considering all of the obstacles for a naturalistic explanation for origins, creation of life by God should remain an option.

NASA has committed significant resources toward looking for life or evidence of life on other planets. In fact, this was one of the research objectives of the Mars rover. Thus far, it has turned up empty. Somewhat ironically, one of the working definitions to identify life in space that was proposed by Carl Sagan is "a chemical system that carries out Darwinian evolution." The assumption of evolution was built into the definition.

Conclusion

Although scientists have sought to explain the origin of life solely through natural laws and processes for decades, all they have really shown are the obstacles that exist for life coming about through chance. Scientists have discovered how some of the key molecules of organisms can be produced naturally, but they cannot make them all. The specificity and the information content in proteins, DNA and RNA cannot arise through random mutations alone.

The attributes of living things, their integrative complexity, interdependence and elegance all bear witness to the Creator who made them. In Romans 1:20, Paul wrote: "For since the creation of the world God's invisible qualities—his eternal power and divine nature—have been clearly seen, being understood from what has been made, so that men are without excuse." Nowhere is this more evident than in the area of the origin of life. Even the smallest, simplest bacterium bears witness to the wisdom of God who made it.

When we view life as precious, as a gift from our Father in heaven, we catch a glimpse of His wisdom and majesty. Life is not an accident, but each creature has a God-given purpose and plan to fulfill. Human life in particular—created in the image of God—has tremendous value. Contrast that with an evolutionary view that life is "a frozen accident" or a "happy coincidence." In evolution, life is cheap and nothing more than molecules in motion. Our Living God has created living things that reveal his glory.

---

[1] Darwin, Charles. 1871. Letter to Joseph Hooker.

[2] Quote is from the speech Louis Pasteur gave to the French Academy of Science when he won the prize for resolving the matter of spontaneous generation.

[3] Ohmoto et al, 2006. "Suphur isotope evidence for an oxic Archaean atmosphere *Nature* **442**:908-911.

12

Evangelism in Athens

"Men of Athens! I see that in every way you are very religious....Now what you worship as something unknown I am going to proclaim to you.

"The God who made the world and everything in it is the Lord of heaven and earth and does not live in temples built by hands...From one man he made every nation of men, that they should inhabit the whole earth; and he determined the times set for them and the exact places where they should live."

Paul the Apostle
Acts 17: 22-26 (NIV)

The Rise and Decline of Christian Europe

The foundation of Christianity in Europe may have been laid by the Apostle Paul. Acts 16 describes Paul's vision of a man from Macedonia which led him to take the gospel to Europe. Paul preached in many cities across Greece. Ultimately he was arrested and brought to Rome. While in Rome, he and others bore witness to the Gospel and many people were brought to faith in Christ. In spite of much persecution, the Christian faith spread throughout the Roman Empire. Within a few centuries, Christianity became the dominant religion across the European continent.

The Christian influence in Europe was very great. Although dominated by the Roman Catholic Church for centuries, Protestantism began in Europe. Martin Luther sparked the Reformation in the 1500's which gave rise to the Lutheran church. Also at this time, John Calvin started the Christian Reformed

223

Church. In England, the Anglican Church split off from the Roman Catholic Church. Many other important Christian leaders and sects also originated in Europe. Because of wars and religious persecution of different Christian sects, some of these people came to North America in pursuit of religious freedom. The Christian roots of the United States are evident throughout the founding documents of the nation.

Since the 1600's and accelerating after the French Revolution, Europe has become increasingly secularized. With the acceptance of Darwin's theory of evolution and the philosophy of Nietzsche, Europeans began to embrace atheistic humanism throughout the last century. **Ideas have consequences and the widespread abandonment of Christianity is no exception.** Fewer and fewer Europeans practice the Christian faith and the number of Muslims has increased. According to recent statistics in England:

> "Holy Week has begun with an expert prediction that the Christian church in this country will be dead and buried within 40 years. It will vanish from the mainstream of British life, with only 0.5 percent of the population attending the Sunday services of any denomination, according to the country's leading church analyst."

> "Dr. Brierley's findings come just five months after the publication of his latest English Church Attendance Survey, an independent study of all denomination. It showed that only 7.5% of the population went to church on Sundays, and that in the past 10 years – billed as the "Decade of Evangelism" – church attendance dropped by an 'alarming' 22 percent"[1]

Along with a decline in the percentage of those that attend church, Europe is experiencing a serious population decline. In order to maintain a population, each woman must have an average of 2.1 children. This is necessary for replacement (mother, father and infant/child mortality) but will not yield an increase in the population. If the birth rate is greater than this, then the population will grow. However, if the birthrate is below this, the population

224

will actually decrease in number. As of 2004, eighteen European countries have birth rates below the population replacement rate. Italy (1.2), Germany (1.3) and Spain (1.1) in particular have rates that are so low that the population is projected to drop by tens of millions of people over the next few decades. Over a generation at such a rate will lead to a population decrease of nearly 1/3. These are not people who have been killed—they are people who were never born.

In *The Cube and the Cathedral,* George Weigel linked the rise of secularization to the demographic decline of Europe. He suggested that with a lack of spirituality, there is also a lack of willingness to sacrifice and hope for the future. Both of these appear necessary for people to *want* to have children. Children would be considered obstacles to those with a commitment to "the good life" above all. Weigel wrote:

> "Both American and European friends and colleagues with whom I have discussed these questions understandably find it hard to accept what they regard as a too simple, even simplistic notion: that Europe has stopped reproducing itself because most Europeans have stopped going to church. And put that baldly, the analysis is too simple. Of course there are economic, sociological, psychological, and even ideological reasons why Europe's birthrates have fallen below replacement level for decades. But the failure to create a human future in the most elemental sense—by creating a successor generation—is surely an expression of a broader failure: a failure of self confidence. That broader failure is no less surely tied to a collapse of faith in the God of the Bible. For when God goes—and the death of the biblical God in the European public square is what today's European actors in the ongoing drama of atheistic humanism seek and have to a significant measure accomplished—so does God's first command: 'Be fruitful and multiply' (Genesis 1:28)."[2]

I agree with Weigel's assessment of the situation in Europe. It would seem that without religious purpose, humanity fails to

225

perform the most basic function of life: reproduction. In a way it is ironic that those who reject God also ignore the first command in Genesis 1 "Be fruitful and increase in number." Although Weigel made that connection, I don't think he went far enough. Weigel attributes the increase in secularism to forgetting the Christian roots of Europe and a distrust of religion in part because of all of the religious wars. Instead, I would attribute it more directly to a rejection of God as Creator and abandonment of the Word of God. Without God, there can be no moral absolutes.

Ken Ham, founder of Answers in Genesis ministries, has often said, "If you reject the Bible's history, you will reject the Bible's morality." Indeed, Jesus himself said, "I have spoken to you of earthly things and you do not believe; how then will you believe if I speak of heavenly things?" (John 3:12 NIV) People will tend to be consistent. If the first eleven chapters of Genesis is viewed as a myth, on what basis is the rest of the Bible to be taken as real history? Jesus said, "As it was in the days of Noah, so it will be at the coming of the Son of Man." (Matthew 24:37 NIV) If the Flood is a myth, then this would argue that the Second Coming is also a myth.

Secularists fail to realize that without a sure foundation and basis for truth and morality, ultimately anything goes. When man sets the rules, the one who is the strongest or has the most money and power will be the one that sets the rules. Words such as "freedom," "right," "noble," and "true" have an elastic meaning if they are not founded upon an absolute standard. True freedom can only be found in Jesus Christ who said, "You shall know the truth and the truth shall set you free." Without an absolute standard, there is no sure basis to discern right from wrong when your freedom encroaches upon mine.

Genesis and the creation account in particular establish a foundation for morality. Because God made the world and everything in it, he sets the rules and the boundaries. God established the value of man by creating him separately from all other creatures and making male and female "in the image of God." God established marriage and the family by creating one man and one woman. God gave man work and charged him with tending the Garden of Eden and exercising dominion and care for

226

all of creation. Without that firm foundation, mankind loses its moral compass. To some extent, many of our churches are responsible because they have failed to teach people that the Bible is real history and relevant to the real world.

"Jews" Vs. "Greeks"

When Peter spoke on Pentecost, he had before him a completely Jewish audience. They all knew the Law, they knew the promises of God and they understood sin. They believed in the one true God and worshipped him alone. Thus, when Peter preached, those who listened had an appropriate framework with which to understand what he was saying. They had the terminology down and it made sense. They knew about the promised Messiah and expected him to come. Peter only had to explain that Jesus was the Christ and that he rose from the dead. Through faith in him, they could have eternal life. The people responded, recognizing their need and asked what they should do to be saved. More than 3,000 were baptized on that day.

Paul received a much different response when he went to Greece. There, people worshipped all kinds of gods and idols. They were quite religious and had temples and altars to just about every god they could think of. In fact, they even had an altar that was labeled "to an unknown god" in case they missed one! It is in this context that Paul approached them.

With respect, Paul began where they were and quoted from their own philosophers. But Paul did not take the same approach that Peter did. Instead, Paul started with creation. Paul told them about the God whom they did not know—the one who does not live in temples built by human hands as if he needed anything. This is the God who made the world and everything in it, the Creator of the entire universe. From there, he went on to mention Adam and then sin. After that he went into redemption.

In order to understand the Gospel, people need to have a context. Without knowing what sin is or why we need a Savior, the Gospel makes no sense. Without recognizing God as Creator, redemption makes no sense. I have confirmed with missionaries to pagan tribes in Africa, that they often use creation as a starting point. They begin by talking about the God who made the mountains and everything else. Often, the people want to learn about this God, and that opens the door for them to be taught.

In some ways, it is ironic that our "civilized," technologically advanced, Western people can be harder to reach than pagan tribesmen. At least the latter know that there is a God who made everything. Increasingly, as our society and world becomes more secularized, the need to start with creation will increase. In the past, Americans had a Biblical knowledge base. Whether people went to church or not, they knew what sin was and knew that they were in trouble. They knew that they needed God although they might not know how to be saved. These people could be reached with the Gospel and John 3:16 was the place to start. However, for people who don't know whether God exists or not and don't have a concept of what sin is, Genesis 1-11 is a better place to start.

How to use Creation Evangelism

The most important thing to remember regarding the origins controversy is that it is really a battle between worldviews. It is not science vs. religion or fact vs. faith. The conflict is over the correct interpretation of the evidence.

1. Expose the Worldview Conflicts

An effective means to help people to see the evidence for creation is to expose conflicting beliefs. I believe that there are certain worldview elements that people hold tighter than others. If a conflict can be shown between a tightly held belief and one that is only loosely held, people will quickly abandon the latter. For example, Christians who claim to believe the Bible yet also believe in billions of years of evolution may not realize the problem of death before sin. I have observed that sharing that fact alone has made a difference to a number of people. Others don't see a conflict between God making all of the creatures during creation week and the dinosaurs dying millions of years before man existed. However, if God made the dinosaurs on Day 6, the same day as man, then this is impossible. Still others believed that God made

228

other people along with Adam and Eve. They simply did not recognize the conflict that results if there are people that are not descendants of Adam and Eve.

When polled, the vast majority of Americans often say that they believe in God. This is true regardless of whether they attend church or have a relationship with Jesus Christ. Many of these people would confess that they believe that God made everything however they also believe in evolution. Such individuals are not too unlike the men in Athens that Paul spoke to—religious and yet they do not really know the God of the Bible. They may have a vague concept of sin but not really understand what the Gospel is about. Just as Paul began with Creation, this is a good place to start. The Gospel can be difficult to understand without knowing about Creation and the Fall. The idea is to help people develop a consistent worldview—one based on the Bible.

The primary goal of creation evangelism is to help people become Christians and come to an understanding of the Gospel of Christ. A second goal is help Christians to have a more consistent worldview based on the Scriptures. With so much exposure to evolution through media, public schools and even some Christian schools, it is no wonder there is confusion and compromise when it comes to origins. Unfortunately, even in many churches, people need a better understanding of the origins controversy from a Biblical perspective. There are also many Christians who believe Genesis but don't know how to defend it. They need to have answers and know the reasons for their faith.

2. Show the Assumptions

Throughout this book, the assumptions for the creation and evolution views have been presented. Often those who believe in evolution are totally unaware of the presuppositions that their beliefs are based on. Instead, they perceive them to be proven scientific facts and as certain as the earth revolving around the sun. Such a view is often promoted in media reports and television programs. Creationists are portrayed as ignorant and blindly following their faith. One of my purposes in writing this book has been to show that faith in the Genesis account of creation is *reasonable* and supported from both a *scientific* and Biblical perspective. When people begin to realize that there are alternative ways of looking at and interpreting data, they are less defensive. Focusing the debate as a competition between assumptions makes for a more even fight. Additionally, since creationists use the Bible as a source of information and presuppositions, it does not have to be excluded from consideration.

3. Stay informed

Staying current on developments in the area of origins is very important. Creationist organizations such as the Institute for Creation Research **www.icr.org** and Answers in Genesis **www.answersingenesis.org** are both excellent sources of information about the origins controversy. They have teams of scientists that research and report on exciting new results that support creation. In addition, they analyze and comment on material produced in support of evolution and provide information from a creation perspective.

Origins related topics are in the news virtually every day. Whether it is a new dinosaur skeleton, a new fossil hominid or alleged genetic links between different species, evolution is frequently in the media. If you stay informed on these issues and can recognize the assumptions they can provide excellent talking points with friends and relatives. These can serve as conversation starters with friends and coworkers that can open the door to sharing about your belief in creation and your relationship with Christ.

4. Don't let the science intimidate you

For too long, many Christians have avoided science. Both because it is a difficult subject and for fear that studying it might cause them to lose their faith. All disciplines and channels of culture need Christians and this is especially true of science. There is nothing intrinsically evil about science and it can be done from a creationist perspective. If there is a particular subject in science that interests you, study it. Learn more about it. My middle

230

daughter was very afraid of bees. One day she told me that she was going to get a book about bees from the library. She thought if she learned more about them, then she wouldn't be as scared. This was very profound for a second grader.

Don't let the degrees intimidate you either. Scientists are people too. They may know a lot, but they don't know everything. Learn to ask probing questions. A good one is simply, "How do you know that?" Sometimes a simple question like that will reveal the assumptions that the work is based on. One of my former students was a communications major with very little training in science. After taking my creation studies course at Liberty University, she talked to a number of evolutionary scientists with Ph.D.s. She was able to cut through the smokescreens and ask questions that ultimately they refused to answer.

From the outside, it would have seemed that David should have been intimidated to go up against the giant, Goliath. However, the God who was with him when he killed the lion and the bear would certainly deliver him from the Philistine. Pray for wisdom from God and he will give it to you. (James 1:5-8)

5. Use Gentleness and Respect

Peter admonished Christians to "always be prepared to give an answer to everyone who asks you to give the reason for the hope that you have, but do this with gentleness and respect." (1 Peter 3:15 NIV) Therefore, it is imperative that we are ready to give answers to people. This includes being ready to discuss creation and defend it. Since origins and related worldview issues are often in the news, many people may want to discuss these subjects. If we are prepared with answers, it can open up a door to discuss our faith in Christ.

The temptation, however, is to turn the discussion into a debate. It is possible to get so caught up in winning an argument, that the whole purpose is lost. Don't win the battle and loose the war. In the heat of the moment it is easy to get sidetracked and feel like you have got to win. The discussion can get heated and go too far. Always remember that you are representing Christ and your gentleness should be evident to all. If you don't know the answer, admit it. It is better to say that you don't know something than give an answer that it incorrect. Your credibility can be damaged. If you make a mistake, correct it at the first opportunity.

Sometimes it is best just to give people something to think about. Ask that probing question, and just leave it at that. They may shoot back a quick answer, but they also will have to think about it. While in graduate school, there was a complicated lecture on the regulation of genes. The professor spent well over an hour explaining how just one gene was turned on and off. The process was truly amazing. At lunch with my fellow students, we were discussing the lecture. One of them raised the question about how such a complex system could possibly evolve. Without missing a beat, I said, "It didn't. God made it." For about 5 seconds there was total silence. Then one of the students laughed and then so did the rest. But for 5 seconds, they thought about it.

At a meeting with a number of other scientists, I met a geologist. This was the first time I had ever met someone with a Ph.D. in geology and so I had a number of questions that I wanted to ask. After that, the discussion turned to the origin of life. I told him that I was a cell biologist, but had a lot of trouble seeing how the science could work for the origin of life. For quite a while, I brought up problem after problem and obstacle after obstacle. Then he said, "You know. Maybe God did it after all." With that, I said, "I can come to no other conclusion and that is why I believe Genesis." I then was able to share my testimony and explain what the Gospel meant. **Don't get so caught up in the origins controversy that the Gospel is left out**.

Some people are evidential doubters. Like Thomas, they need to see the evidence. They need to put their finger in the scars from the nails. Help them to see. Open their eyes so that they can interpret the evidence from a creation view. They might not see that "proof" that they so desperately want, however, you might be able to help them walk by faith and not by sight.

6. Understand the problem of evil

One of the most common obstacles to faith in Christ is probably the "problem of evil." It takes many forms, but a typical one is:

232

"If God is real then why did.... happen?" Often there is a serious tragedy in the person's life and they blame God for it. Darwin's daughter Annie died at the age of eight years old. When this happened, any vestige of faith remaining in him probably died too. I have heard many stories like this of how people lose their faith after the death of a loved one. Since they can't really blame God, they conclude that God doesn't exist.[3]

Death is ugly. It is probably one of the worst things that we can experience as human beings. But as bad as death is, there is something worse—spending eternity separated from God in Hell. Unfortunately, death is necessary in a fallen world. Death is necessary because it is the only way for us to be able to be redeemed. It is through the death of Jesus, that those of us who have faith in him will be able to inherit eternal life. The good news is that death is not the end. We will see our loved ones who died in the Lord again.

Death really is an intrusion into this world. It came as the wages of sin when our first father Adam rebelled against God. For evolution, death has been ever present and is the means by which new species arise through natural selection. This is where the theory of evolution cuts to the foundation of the Gospel. Jesus came to defeat death and it is called "the last enemy." This world is one that is filled with death, disease and pain. But in the world to come they will be no more.

The world we live in is one that has been cursed by God. The ground produces "thorns and thistles." We must live "by the sweat of our brow." Dust we are and to dust we shall return. This problem of evil in the world is one that man caused in the first place. But thanks be to God! He has redeemed us and freed us from the power of death so that it no longer holds sting for us.

7. Trust the Word

One of the most important things that a Christian can do is to trust the Bible. When we don't understand or when the evidence seems to point in the opposite direction, it can be especially difficult to believe the Word. However, it is at those times that it is also the most crucial. While I was in college and believed God used evolution to create, what helped me was recognizing the importance of the Scriptures. Jesus believed the Scriptures and quoted from them repeatedly. He submitted to them and followed them. Who am I to say which portions are true and which are not? Although I believe that scientific evidence supports a creation view, I do not base my belief on that evidence but on the Word.

Often, the media hypes some new hominid ancestor or any number of evidences that mankind evolved from chimp-like ancestors.[4] The evidence can seem persuasive or even compelling. I have experienced this enough times to know that all I have to do is wait. After a while, some new evidence will cast doubt on what once seemed incontrovertible evidence for evolution. Sometimes all it takes is a more critical look at the same evidence.[5] But even if I don't find the solution, I will still put my hope and trust in my Creator. My faith is in the Word of God and not the scientific evidence.

Conclusion

This book began with a trip to Washington D.C. and the contrast between an evolution and a creation worldview. Creation and evolution are two different ways of looking at the world and answering the question: "Where did all of this come from?" As has been discussed, the assumptions that are used to interpret the data ultimately play a major role in determining the conclusions that will be reached. Throughout this book I have presented those assumptions for both sides in order to unravel the origins controversy.

It is my sincere hope and prayer that this book has encouraged you to have more confidence in the Bible. I hope that it has helped you to look more critically at the evidence used to support evolution and equipped you to better defend a creation point of view. If you are not a Christian, I hope that this book has challenged you to learn more about Jesus Christ.

> "In the beginning was the Word, and the Word was with God, and the Word was God. He was with God in the beginning. Through him all things were made; without him

234

nothing was made that has been made....He was in the world, and though the world was made through him, the world did not recognize him. He came to that which was his own, but his own did not receive him. Yet to all who received him, to those who believed in his name, he gave the right to become children of God—children born not of natural descent, nor of human decision or a husband's will, but born of God. The Word became flesh and made his dwelling among us. We have seen his glory, the glory of the One and Only who came from the Father, full of grace and truth." (John 1:1-3, 10-14, NIV)

---

[1] Church 'will be dead in 40 years time' Independent.co.uk 16 April 2003

[2] Weigel, George 2005. *The Cube and the Cathedral*, Basic Books, New York pp 164.

[3] For an excellent and current treatment of this subject, Ken Ham's book "*How Could a Loving God...? Powerful Answers on Suffering*" Published by Answers in Genesis—US 2006.

[4] For example, this article from TIME magazine: Lemonick, M.D. and Dorfman, A. What *makes us different?* TIME October 1, 2006.
http://www.time.com/time/magazine/article/0,9171,1541283,00.html

[5] DeWitt, David A. *TIME to stay current on human origins* Oct 2, 2006.
http://www.answersingenesis.org/docs2006/1002time.asp

About the Author

Dr. David A. DeWitt is the Director of the Center for Creation Studies and a Professor of Biology at Liberty University. He received his Bachelor of Science degree in Biochemistry from Michigan State University and a Ph.D. in Neurosciences from Case Western Reserve University. Currently, he is active in both teaching and research. His primary research efforts have been to understand the mechanisms causing cellular damage in Alzheimer's disease. He has authored and co-authored articles that have appeared in peer-reviewed journals such as *Experimental Neurology* and the *Journal of Alzheimer's Disease*. His research was funded by an Academic Research Enhancement Award from the National Institutes of Health. He teaches undergraduate courses in Cell Biology and Biochemistry as well as two courses on the origins controversy. He is an adjunct faculty member of the Institute for Creation Research in San Diego and a frequent writer/speaker for Answers in Genesis. Liberty University recognized Dr. DeWitt with the 2000-2001 President's Award for Teaching Excellence.